AMERICAN WOMAN

Lost and Found
in Oklahoma

Pam Fleischaker

FULL CIRCLE PRESS : OKLAHOMA CITY

Printed and bound in the United States of America

Book, text, and jacket designed by Carl Brune.

Edited by Shauna Lawyer Struby.

Published by Full Circle Press, a division of Full Circle Bookstore,
50 Penn Place, Oklahoma City, OK 73118

ISBN 0-9661460-1-8

For David, Joey and Emily
sunshine when skies are gray

CONTENTS

ONE

PROMS, PENNY-LOAFERS AND OTHER PRIVILEGES

TWO

OK BY ME

ACKNOWLEDGEMENTS

I n compiling this book, I have had a wonderful cheering section of friends and family, many of whom were early readers of the drafts. Thanks to Anne Barnstone, J.B. Bleckley, Ellen Feuerborn, Joie Singer, Deborah Lynch, Mimi Mager and Marcy Roberts for the thumbs-up to keep moving.

Susan Estrich read and re-read, gave me valuable insights and told me, as she always does, to go for it. My buddies Phil Bacharach and Toby Thompson are both terrific writers who also read early drafts and put up with my constant requests for advice. Mary Corson wins the prize for the most ideas on the back of an envelope and Jon Sackler wins the sickest title entry award. Janet Wilson is always there for me no matter how badly I behave, with tough talk and a great meal, and Tom Wilson helps me see things more clearly.

Kevin Sullivan has been putting words into other people's mouths for years, and we all sound better for it. I thank him, as ever, for his help.

Bill Bleakley, owner and publisher of the Oklahoma Gazette, has provided me and others at the paper with the freedom and the forum to write what I believe, and I am grateful to him for his support.

Mike Easterling, editor of the Oklahoma Gazette and my good friend for more than a decade, taught me to be a journalist. He taught me to put my thoughts into honest, and fewer, words; to make my opinions count for something; to write from my heart and never be a wimp in the face of authority. Never.

Jim Tolbert, the brains behind Full Circle Bookstore and Full Circle Press, is a man of great class and integrity. I can't imagine a finer publisher and guide. Shauna Struby has been a gentle but prodding editor, who helped me get over my unnatural attachment to parentheses. Carl Brune is a talented artist and designer, always open to my ideas and vision.

Debbie Fleischaker has worked overtime on me for 30 years. Her intellectual input is important, but mostly it's the jewelry. I'd be unadorned without her.

Missy Mandell lost all her eye make-up reading an early version of this book on an airplane. Her comments and suggestions were, without exception, on target. Her editing notes go in my keepsake box forever. But mostly, her pride and enthusiasm in my accomplishments are a great gift. But I'm not surprised. There really never were such devoted sisters.

I learned everything I needed to know from Bud and Dottie Mandell. They put the music in my life.

And David Fleischaker, my best friend, has read everything I've written 'til his hair has fallen out. When I get cold feet, he warms them. He can always be counted on for the smartest, sharpest and most honest feedback. Even when he's wrong.

FOREWORD

Former President William J. Clinton

F rom the first time I met Pam Fleischaker, I knew she was comfortable with who she was and certain of her values.

We first met more than 30 years ago in Washington, D.C. I was a summer intern about to start law school. She was new to the East Coast, new to Washington and new to politics. She had taken a job with Common Cause, the citizens' lobby newly established to reform the already-broken campaign finance system.

Common Cause was a natural magnet for high-energy, ambitious, young progressives in the Nixon years. I had a lot of friends working at Common Cause, people with whom I had worked in various political campaigns, and it was at a party thrown by some of these friends that I met Pam. We have maintained our friendship over all the years since.

From our first conversation it was clear she was not your typical up-and-coming politico. She had worked as a fashion copywriter for Neiman-Marcus in Dallas, a job she loved, she was quick to add. So how did you end up at Common Cause? I asked. Mostly luck, she replied. She suspected she got the job because she told interviewers she loved to type and would do anything to help.

When I returned to Arkansas to run for public office, Pam remained in Washington, working in the vanguard of groups advancing congressional reform and assisting women running for political office.

In 1981, Pam left Washington and moved to Oklahoma with her family, but she remained involved in national politics. Our paths crossed often in the 1984 Mondale-Ferraro presidential campaign and again in 1988, in the Dukakis-Bentsen presidential effort. While we worked in more losing campaigns than I care to remember — including my own for Congress in 1974 — we shared a lot of common goals and good times.

In the Nineties, Pam began a new career as a columnist, writing for the Oklahoma Gazette in Oklahoma City.

In this collection taken from her weekly columns, you'll find her goading a reluctant Republican governor to enact sensible gun control laws, exposing the journalistic mediocrity of the city's powerful right-wing daily newspaper and challenging those who would limit a woman's control over her body and destiny.

At the same time, she is a voice of reconciliation, appealing to those in her community — a predominantly white, conservative Christian community — to understand and be tolerant of those who are different, whether their difference is one of race, religion or sexual orientation.

One week Pam is upbraiding the self-appointed censors who would, in God's name, ban books from students' reading lists, and the next she is extolling the common virtues of the people in her community who still have time for simple expressions of decency.

And there is more: Pam revisiting the angst of her adolescence, recording her children's passages, extolling the virtues of *foie gras*, chocolate and shopping. Her range of commentary runs from Martha Stewart to Barry Bonds, from the First Amendment to the first date.

What makes this good reading is that Pam has an instinct for the unadorned, unvarnished truth. She speaks simply and honestly about her feelings. Add to that a large capacity for compassion, a rollicking sense of humor, stir in a little mischief and you have my friend, Pam.

As you read these pieces, you'll find yourself thinking, "I remember feeling that way" and thinking that she's got it right. And you will find yourself laughing, laughing a lot.

Bill Clinton

February 2001

AUTHOR'S NOTE

Where you live is not important, wise people told me.

It's how you live that counts.

Still, I felt as though I was stepping off a cliff blindfolded as I readied myself in 1981 for a move from Washington, D.C. — where I had lived for nearly 12 years from my mid-twenties to mid-thirties — to Oklahoma City, my husband's hometown. Something I suspected about "place" worried me about this move.

I think place matters. I think that where you are has a lot to do with how you are. Where I would live — how it would look and smell, its energy, its taste, its history, its personality, its culture — all of that mattered to me, as I prepared to make a home in a town I would call my hometown.

Oklahoma City was then much like it is today. People were friendly and open. You could see all of the sky all of the time. The air was clear, the traffic was negligible. Lovely houses with big yards in nice neighborhoods were affordable and life was easy.

But for me, the change was a setback. I imagined I would never click with Oklahomans. In Washington, I had been schooled in assertive, activist, left-wing advocacy, thrived on it, in fact, and was afraid I would stick out like a sore, liberal thumb in laid-back Oklahoma.

Initially, I crossed paths with very few women who worked in Oklahoma City, even fewer who were passionate about their work. I sought out activists, but they were few and far between. Oklahoma's politics was full of good ol' boys (actually, good ol' men), corrupt county commissioners and a few bright lights, who, by then, were burning out. The media was, and is, The Daily Oklahoman, a big, domineering statewide newspaper run by a wealthy conservative family whose attitude seems to be keep 'em uninformed, barefoot and pregnant, and they won't ever want to leave the farm.

Yet it was in Oklahoma City that I eventually found deeply satisfying work and raised a strong, healthy family. I found as colleagues a group of smart, hard-working women and men dedicated to helping women and their families.

I always believed I was making a contribution in Washington, but it was hard to see. After months of killing work, my candidate always lost the White House, and those I'd help elect to Congress were swallowed up in the next election by another candidate with more money.

I began noticing — now with a more observant, less personal eye — what was available and what was missing in this city I was calling home, and I began writing about it, all of it. Politics, kids, husbands, being out when you wanted in, being in when it didn't work out. At first, I wrote mostly for myself and really to myself. Seeing it on paper helped me sort out what mattered and what didn't, where I was and why.

My point of view as a woman, a liberal, a Jew, an insider who always felt out, mattered to me more and more, particularly as that viewpoint was under-represented in the city.

I have tried to provoke and have certainly been provoked. I have tried to keep my topics, my writing and myself lively.

From the death of my much-loved mother, to my son's graduation, my daughter's coming of age and my husband's mid-life pursuits, I have tried to understand living by writing about it.

From the excitement and pride at seeing Bill Clinton, an old friend and political ally, elected President of the United States, to the confusion at his fall from grace, I have tried to understand national politics in America in the 21st Century by writing about it.

From the perspective of a Jewish woman living in an overwhelmingly Christian community, I have tried to gain, and regain, my footing by writing about it.

From the inhumanity of a city commission's actions against its gay community to a terrifying act of domestic terrorism and destruction, I have tried to understand living in Oklahoma City by writing about it.

I have engendered enthusiasm and criticism for my positions. I have gotten phone calls, letters, e-mail and hate mail.

"Go for it, Pam!" one fellow wrote. "You're a light in the darkness."

"Go to hell, you damned liberal," wrote someone else.

Where you are does matter.

And here I am. Writing to myself, and for those like and unlike me from a place in the very middle of America.

I write from the place I hold as an American woman — a mother, a wife, an activist. I write from the extraordinary place of being an American at the turn of a fast-paced, high-tech century, an Oklahoman with an East Coast attitude and an outsider with an insider's moxie. In the frantic world of American political life, in the zigzagging but joyful refuge of my family and in the red earth of Oklahoma, I found a place.

May 2001

Getting here from there

THE LAND OF NON-PERSPIRING BLONDES

A full-fledged Baby Boomer, I was born in 1946 to Bud and Dottie Mandell, who were struggling to make it in the post-war, rough and tumble oil and gas business in Texas. For the first 10 years of my life, my cheerful, optimistic and hard-working parents dragged my sister, Missy, and me all over the state from small, dusty towns that barely supported a truckload of oil field workers and a few "executives" (office boys), to bigger boom towns just beginning to shine, like Houston, Austin and Dallas.

I spent all of my adolescence in Dallas, sweltering in the heat, secure in what was a uniquely happy and close-knit family, but never feeling I fit in with the broader community.

All around me were pretty, pert blondes and big, beefy guys. In the way that only tortured adolescents can, I imagined these North Dallas girls lived in grand houses, wore clothes with the right labels, had sex with their boyfriends behind church social halls and had tan, unblemished skin all year long. That was actually not just my imagination. That was North Dallas in the Sixties.

In this Land of Non-perspiring Blondes, I was a moody, big-featured, dark-haired Jewish girl who loved to dance and write. I liked conversation with smart, quick, nerdy boys, not driving around in the back of a hot, windy convertible lookin' for Bobby Lee and the rest of the defensive line. I had a few oddball friends who felt as out of place as I did, and I knew, as young as age 13, that this was the wrong place for me.

College at the University of Colorado, then at the University of Texas in Austin, was better. Finding some comfortable places for myself, I worked on the campus newspaper and became involved in student politics. Proudly, I marched to the steps of the Texas state Capitol against the war in Vietnam in 1968. Admiringly, I worked alongside my boyfriend (now husband) who was the brainy one in law school, the leader of the human rights club.

Still, I felt I was pushing from the outside, never really to be in. Maybe it was the heat; maybe the attitudes; maybe it was my attitude. I could hardly wait to leave.

FINDING MY PLACE

At 22, when the brainy-boyfriend-husband, David, and I moved to Washington, D.C. (for his job, of course, but I quickly found one), I came alive.

With luck, I landed a post with a group of young political activists working for Common Cause, a citizens' lobby committed to election law and campaign finance reform. We — oh, how I loved using that word we — worked to pass an amendment giving 18-year-olds the right to vote and brought lawsuits to make campaigning and lobbying more open and above board. And like almost every other activist group in Washington in the late Seventies, we proudly and aggressively opposed the war in Vietnam.

My boss and mentor then — and my good friend now — was Anne Wexler, a then-fortysomething woman who had been a key player in several Democratic presidential and U.S. Senate campaigns. Like a powerful incarnation of the Pied Piper, she convinced her small staff of young reformers and political organizers that we could, and should, do anything we believed in.

Our band of earnest advocates eventually spread out in two Democratic presidential campaigns — Ed Muskie's and, when that failed, George McGovern's. We worked ridiculously hard, because we believed the political system needed us, because we were ambitious and thought we could change at least some part of the world, because we were young and because it was fun. Really fun.

BIG SHOTS AT 25

I felt I had finally found my place — outside government but inside the world of political activism. For the next 10 years I continued working for political advocacy groups against the war in Vietnam, for the right to choose abortion, for ratification of the Equal Rights Amendment, for public financing of elections and for women running for public office.

I was involved in Democratic campaigns like Geraldine Ferraro's first bid for Congress in New York; Bill Clinton's unsuccessful bid for Congress from Arkansas; Tom Harkin's first run for Congress from Iowa; Barbara Mikulski's first race for the U.S. Senate from Maryland.

On one particularly wild ride in 1972, my husband and I, my sister, Wexler and her husband Joseph Duffey, and no more than about 10 other 20ish-year-olds, put on a national Democratic issues convention in Louisville, Ky., with 2,000 delegates, 500 members of the national press corps and seven Democratic presidential candidates. We thought we were running the world.

Chutzpah? You bet. In over our heads? Certainly. But we were passionate, committed and willing to work ourselves to the bone. At 25, we were big shots.

In those years in Washington, I cut my teeth, professionally, on helping public servants who did good, honest work in politics. That system has gone sour for most, but it never went sour for me.

I knew then, and still know today, men and women in both political parties and at all levels of government who work hard and with integrity for the public they serve. By dint of my own abilities and my willingness to work, I finally understood the satisfaction and the responsibilities of being an insider. And I have not lost my faith in America or its madcap systems of law-making and governing.

DO I GET A TURN?

By the time I was 30, I wanted a family and a less frenetic pace. I took a job as an associate political producer for CBS News in Washington during the election period of 1976 and thrived again.

I saw candidates, issues and politicians from the other side, from the perspective of the media covering their campaigns. I wrote for correspondents and producers and loved it.

Our son, Joey, was born the next year, and while I stayed in the political media game in Washington, directing my professional energy toward electing women in both parties to office, my priorities had changed. I wanted to be home more and tried, with uneven success, to balance my growing professional life with the needs of my growing child. It was, and is, the hardest work I've ever done.

In 1981, my husband decided to leave his career as an environmental attorney in Washington and return to take up the reins of a family oil and gas business in Oklahoma. For two years, while our son grew from 2 to 4, my husband commuted between his business in Oklahoma City and our home and family in Washington. I kept "doing politics," taking care of our son and trying to be supportive of David's absences. Lots of people had commuting marriages, we said to each other; we'd manage, too.

But in fact, it was awful — an impossible way to conduct a relationship and no way to run a family or two careers. So I packed up and we moved.

TWO PLACES AT ONCE

Now I had one foot in Oklahoma, the other in Washington, and was looking for the best way to bridge the gap for myself.

The right to choose safe and legal abortion was seriously at risk in Oklahoma in the early Eighties, and I immediately saw ways I could help.

For many years, I worked for Planned Parenthood of Central Oklahoma, lobbying in the state Legislature and growing the ranks of supporters in the central part of the state. When I was seven months pregnant with our daughter, I stood before a state Senate committee and persuaded enough members to vote against a severe abortion restriction to defeat the measure.

In Washington, D.C., while the issue is attacked legally and through national policy, it is always at a distance. Weeks of work with the staff of a congressional committee might change one word in one line of a bill about family planning funds, only to be used as a political ploy to defeat some other issue. Presidential vetoes and the U.S. Supreme Court are the battlegrounds for fighting for abortion rights at that level.

In Oklahoma, the hostility toward those of us advocating the preservation of this legal procedure was, and is, palpable. It takes more than hard work and dedication to buck the majority in the Bible Belt — it takes moxie, and I am proud to say, I knew how to use it.

In slow-moving, stubborn Oklahoma, my ability to persuade one person to vote no on one legislative committee made the difference in preserving personal medical decisions for thousands of women.

Work, career and passion finally merged for me in the heartland, bringing a sense of accomplishment I thought I'd left behind for good.

Someone reminded me recently that life is not one thing after another. It's the same damn thing over and over again.

So it goes with family planning and abortion rights. That fight has to be fought over and over again. I was glad to be in it then, and I'm glad now.

HOW YA GONNA KEEP 'EM DOWN ON THE FARM?

In spite of the gratifying work I was doing in Oklahoma, I missed the energy and excitement of national politics.

So in the national election of 1984, barely retired from nursing our newborn, Emily, I worked for and traveled with Geraldine Ferraro, the

Democratic nominee for vice president and the first woman on a presidential ticket. A woman was running. It was an historic, ground-breaking event and I wanted to be part of it. I bunked in with my friends Wexler and Duffey, and worked as Ferraro's liaison with women and women's organizations, a job that was exhilarating, important, fun and exhausting.

This time, I was the weekend commuter with two kids at home. After we lost that election — my Democrats were batting 0 for 3 — I came home, both to my family and Oklahoma Planned Parenthood.

I geared up again for Mike Dukakis' race for president in 1988, commuting between Boston and Oklahoma. I worked in the campaign's communications office, writing the candidate's responses and trying to persuade the media — yes, spin — to see and report the campaign our way.

I enjoyed this process, a new one for me, different from my feminist-driven legislative advocacy work. I was fascinated with the reporter's difficult task of sorting out the facts from the line skillfully crafted by a campaign, and with the campaign staff's difficult task of packaging and sending a candidate's image, positions and responses. However, unlike Ferraro's "first woman" campaign and my privileged role in that, candidate Dukakis wasn't up to the task and neither was I. As ever, I enjoyed working with a team of bright, committed political co-workers, led by Susan Estrich, the campaign's able manager and my good friend. But on the campaign trail, neither the candidate nor I seemed to know what city we were in or why. We lost, and I came home.

Four presidential campaigns, a lot of liberal doing good, two kids and a husband who supported it all but struggled to keep the family's equilibrium. I was finally getting some perspective.

The balancing act between career and family was killing me. Presidential politics was for young people who could live on powdered sugar donuts and liked the game more than the reasons for playing. My kids needed me, and I needed them. While I still didn't fit into any obvious role in Oklahoma, I was ready to be somewhere I could call home.

HANGING MY HAT

Back in Oklahoma City, I threw myself into volunteer work. I served Planned Parenthood on its board; I participated in a leadership training course for the city; I helped Democrats run for office and was appointed to the city's short-lived Human Rights Commission. I was always drawn to the outsider's fight, the rights of the individual, the defense of the exiled, the cause of the underdog, not a point of view easily or often voiced in Oklahoma City.

"You need a woman's voice on this paper," I said to my friend Randy Splaingard, the editor of the Oklahoma Gazette in the Eighties. "And I don't mean pie recipes and costume-making," I added, although I have happily written about both.

I meant writing about things traditionally done by men in Oklahoma, like politics and lobbying, religion and reform, and being taken seriously for it.

AN ALTERNATIVE FOR ME AND OKLAHOMA CITY

The Oklahoma Gazette is an alternative weekly newspaper launched in 1979 by owner and publisher Bill Bleakley. His worthwhile goal was to provide a compilation of arts and entertainment events, in-depth news reporting, good humor, good writing and an open forum for ideas. This kind of paper was, and still is, sorely needed in a news black hole left by the existing daily paper, The Daily Oklahoman, and was met with tremendous enthusiasm and success.

In 1987, I began writing a weekly commentary column for the Gazette called "At Liberty." Eventually, I joined the staff of the paper as senior associate editor and writer. Today, the Gazette's circulation is 56,000, and it is, without question, the only beacon of journalistic light in central Oklahoma.

For 14 years — as I raised a family, remained involved in my community and confronted my own transformation from young, headstrong activist to older and wiser activist — I have written for the Gazette, supported by tremendous intellectual and artistic freedom. I worked with other excellent writers, conceptualizing and editing stories alongside Mike Easterling, an editor and comrade-in-arms whose judgment, integrity, work ethic and keen eye for fairness are unexcelled in our region. His support, encouragement and respect made it possible for me to grow as a writer and editor, as well as make a contribution to our community.

The paper and its role in Oklahoma City have been my outlet and my inlet, my way of thinking out loud. I have written, re-written and published the column for more than 10 years. This collection represents only a few from those years, with some columns presented as they were originally published and others given background or explanation in a prologue or epilogue. The date under each column's title was its original publication date in the Gazette; the prologues and epilogues were written for this book.

The columns — a home site for some, bird-cage liner for others — have given me, and I hope my neighbors in Oklahoma City, the liberty to think, write and talk about public and private issues. They have given me a new career, a way to re-invent myself, and a chance to write about culture and cuisine, people and politics, family and feminism, things serious and things, at times, very silly.

May 2001

ONE

PROMS, PENNY-LOAFERS AND OTHER PRIVILEGES

PROM NIGHT
MAY 1988

964. Beatles. Big Hair. Bourbon on the Rocks. Boys, boys, boys, boys, boys.

My prom night approaches, and I don't have A Date. It's amazing that I'm actually willing to admit it, though I feel sure that everyone in the Lone Star state has noticed. My best friend, Valerie, knows for sure, because she doesn't Have One either and is likewise consumed with The Shame Of It All. My parents certainly know because my usual adolescent obnoxiousness has reached a new high.

I am one tormented teen.

"Don't worry, honey," my mom says lovingly, but oh, so naively. "There's still a month left. Someone will call."

I glare at both my parents. How can two people be so useless?

The weeks go by. I stalk the halls at school, sizing up any hopefuls but trying not to look too desperate. I feel an enormous arrow must be dangling above my head, following me everywhere, pointing down at me as if to say, "Her! Her! There's one! No one has asked Her yet!"

Now, one week to go and still no calls. I closet myself in my bedroom and stare at the phone which has grown so large it seems to fill every inch of my pink-and-white gingham French-provincial room. And speaking of pink princesses, they all have dates, every last one of them.

"You and Valerie could go together," suggests my mom, leaping years ahead with a very liberated idea. But I was horrified at one more reminder that she really didn't get it.

Things have changed for some prom-goers, and many girls do go with a girlfriend or in groups. Some brave souls even go alone. Their courage astounds and delights me.

But here in Oklahoma City at Putnam City West High School, things actually got worse for a while. For several years, they had an unfortunate policy that required students to attend the prom "with a member of the opposite sex" or not at all.

Had I waited for someone of the oppose sex to pluck me from the vast garden of gorgeous blossoms, I would surely have withered on the vine.

Now that 30 years have passed, one P.C. West student took on the issue, claiming the policy infringed on her rights. You bet it does. I'd say it infringes on her whole adolescence. Asking and fearing the dreaded response, "Well, uh, I don't think . . .," has always been a painful position for both boys and girls, so why force them into it?

We tell them to grow up, be independent, accept responsibility for your own actions, resist the temptations of the crowd and think for yourself — except, of course, in this small matter of your social life and its pinnacle event. In this case, what you do must depend entirely on someone else. Someone else of the opposite sex, yet. Either put yourself heavily on the line, the message is, or stay home. This policy could create an entire generation of agoraphobics who can't leave the house unless they get The Big Call and a corsage.

But you must be dying to hear the end of my story. I simply could not stay home and watch one more Bing Crosby movie with my dad, so I took matters into my own hands.

"Ricky?" I said when my friend in Fort Worth answered the phone.

"Would you be able to come over — I lived in Dallas — and go to my prom with me?"

Ricky Rapfogel. A nice enough guy when he wasn't buried in Kafka or the College Board Study Guide. His dad would let him use the car. He looked perfectly fine. He could be talked into dancing from time to time, and he wasn't that much shorter than I was.

At first, silence from Ricky's end. Then, "What do I have to wear?"

"A tux." I wanted to add "dummy," but some wise voice told me to curb my sarcastic tongue for once.

"Sure," he said. "Why not? See you."

Saved, once again, by a member of the opposite sex.

EPILOGUE

Someone related to Ricky Rapfogel's mother has a cousin who has a niece whose daughter is married to a guy whose sister-in-law lives in Oklahoma City.

Still with me?

She sent Ricky a copy of this column from the Oklahoma Gazette and Ricky tracked me down. We spent 45 minutes on the phone, catching up on years of what's-what, and who married who and who's kids are where. Now we exchange greeting cards and occasional phone calls, and I'm glad to have him back.

He's a psychiatrist in a big city in the Midwest, and when I started blathering all of the above to him, he wisely said we shouldn't overcomplicate the cultural and developmental aspects of it. Mostly, he said, he'd been glad to go with me to the Hillcrest High School prom in Dallas 36 years ago.

"Really?" I replied, still incredulous.

"Yeah."

That Ricky.

"It was a lot of fun." he said.

❧

READY OR NOT

NOVEMBER 1989

H e was riding his bike home, I was out for my afternoon walk, and our paths happened to cross. Since he was juggling a lot — books, a basketball, his costume for the school play — his bike swerved and bumped into me if I walked too close. But if I kept a comfortable distance, it was a nice journey and we both enjoyed the company.

My son is nearly 13 and soon he will become Bar Mitzvah, an important and joyous ritual in our Jewish faith. It means "keeper of the commandments" and is a time when Jewish young men are invited, and expected, to share the responsibilities and privileges of the adult community.

For the first time, they are asked to read the Torah — God's laws or the first five books of the Old Testament — before the entire community and are given the responsibility for keeping them. Not until age 13 is it believed a child is able to accept this awesome task. Learning to read Hebrew and understanding the meaning of the prayers is hard work. Before 13, it's just too hard. But now, at the threshold of manhood, it's time to begin.

"Begin" because it is only a beginning. He is not a boy one day and a man the next. He is not oblivious to the law one day and mindful of it the next. He is beginning to become a man, beginning to understand the ancient teachings of his family's faith and beginning to struggle with his own choices.

And I am just beginning to accept his coming manhood. I cannot truthfully say, "Why, it was just yesterday when my baby boy . . .," because it wasn't. A lot of territory has been covered in 13 years.

He is an active, intense, super-charged guy with a warm heart, a gentle spirit and a pack of talent. He grabs life — usually in the form of a baseball, soccer ball, balletic leap or basketball — and wrestles with it, kicks it, slams it, practices it and finally conquers it. His path is not yet a smooth one.

My instinct, as his mother, is to try to smooth the way, slow the pace, intercept the fast pass and wind down the pitch. If I help him with the responsibilities and rough spots, I sometimes reason, look at how much more he'll enjoy the rewards.

But I cannot slow him down, nor would I. Time is flying, and so is he. As he races past me into adulthood, I can only be there, and not too close at that. If I keep my distance, maybe he'll keep bumping into me.

Just step back and watch, mom, even when he fumbles, overshoots, pitches wild or falls. His job is to begin to accept the responsibilities of his coming manhood, in Judaism and in all of life. Your job is to let him.

Because ready or not, here he comes.

A MILLION MOMS
May 2000

PROLOGUE

Violent gun deaths and injuries in American schools have become our worst nightmare. As we watched terrified students streaming out of Columbine High School in Littleton, Colo.; Paducah, Ky.; Jonesboro, Ark.; Santee, Calif., and other places, our national anxiety about guns in the hands of angry, disturbed or just experimenting students has grown.

As complicated and confusing as the issues are that contribute to a child's violent behavior, it is undeniable that guns in America are increasingly accessible to kids and increasingly present in schools.

The battles over the "right to bear arms," to carry concealed weapons, to register weapons, license weapons, buy and use weapons and attach safety locks to weapons go on and on. In the 2000 presidential election, the Republicans made no excuse for their opposition to gun control and skirted the issue. The Democrats waffled and gave few, if any suggestions, except to give lip service to ending school violence. Both parties, presumably, were cowed by the strength of gun control opponents in the National Rifle Association. Forty percent of those who voted for George W. Bush are gun owners.

If there are solutions, they remain hidden, a metaphor for the illegal and fatal use of guns themselves.

Twelve children die from gunshot wounds in America every day.

Every day. Twelve children.

"Our children's lives far outweigh the right for just anyone, especially juveniles, to carry a semi-automatic assault weapon or Saturday Night Special," said the organizers of the Million Mom March.

"We, the mothers, know that life is the first inalienable right promised by our Constitution."

Seems obvious, doesn't it? Obvious that we would value the lives of our children above nearly anything else in our society. Obvious that protecting them should be a priority for mothers, fathers, lawmakers, business people and government leaders. But more glaringly obvious are the frightening stories of violent gun injuries and deaths of children — Jonesboro, Ark.; Paducah, Ky.; Littleton, Colo.; Flint, Mich.; on and on.

As public sentiment for sensible gun laws has grown, so has the strength of the pro-gun lobby in Congress, opposing nearly every reasonable protection or restriction of gun use considered. In the meantime, remember 12 children die every day.

When one child took a gun from home and killed another in Flint, Mich; when television footage of the Granada Hills Day Camp massacre in California played terrifyingly in our homes; when a 4-year-old took a gun to school thinking it was a toy here in Oklahoma; when Americans began crying enough, one woman in New Jersey decided to take action.

The result of her organizing efforts, and millions like hers, is the Million Mom March, a grassroots effort of mothers, grandmothers and honorary mothers to converge on Washington, D.C., on Mother's Day, 2000, to influence lawmakers to act now for the future safety of all our children. Hundreds of thousands of women and their families are planning the rally on the National Mall and, concurrently, in cities across the country.

On Sunday, May 14, Oklahomans for Gun Safety will lead a march along Riverside Drive in Tulsa. While Rosie O'Donnell, the mother of three, is emceeing the march in Washington, Tulsa Mayor and mom Susan Savage will lead Tulsa's event, along with Lori Hoffner, a Columbine parent.

"The Million Mom March is not about banning guns," the group's organizing materials state. "[It] is about common sense gun laws, specifically urging Congress to enact a law requiring that all gun owners be licensed and registered, including mandatory safety training."

In Oklahoma, legislation mandating minimum gun safety (safety triggers and lock boxes) never even made it out of committee. With the help of state Sen. Maxine Horner, D-Tulsa, the Tulsa gun safety group has made it a priority to move this measure forward in the next session, but this group needs help — your help, my help and help especially from our state leaders.

Why is this so hard? A new study from UCLA found that when a gun and a child are present in a home, 43 percent of the time that gun is not locked up. Safety measures seem a simple enough beginning toward solving this problem, something a popular, Republican governor might easily get behind.

Gov. Keating, (Frank Keating, governor of Oklahoma) I have no doubt of your commitment to ending school violence and applaud your recent conference to examine some solutions, but how can you accomplish that daunting task without addressing the gun problem?

What a wonderful sight it would be, Governor, if you, along with your kids' mom, Cathy, joined those marching in Tulsa and showed your support for ending gun violence.

My family is taking me to Tulsa for Mother's Day. Want to come along? We need your leadership — and that of the state Legislature and congressional delegation — to protect our kids. We need you to join your constituents who want enforcement of existing gun laws and the enactment of more sensible safety measures.

Today, my kids are safe. What I wish for Mother's Day is that yours are, too.

EPILOGUE

My family and our neighbors drove to Tulsa on Mother's Day, marching along with several thousand others to speak out for gun safety. On the National Mall in Washington, D.C., and in hundreds of other American cities, more than a million marched, as well. Neither Gov. Frank Keating of Oklahoma nor members of his family attended.

MOM'S RIGHT

MAY 1990

So sure was my mother that black-suede penny loafers would ruin my feet, I was forbidden to wear them.

Every other seventh-grade girl at Ben Franklin Junior High in Dallas — that's 250 girls, 500 feet — had at least one pair. They were the thing that assured your status, marking you as "in" or, in my case, "out." I never owned a single pair.

Instead, I wore black and white saddle oxfords. They were, my mother sensibly proffered, sturdy and reasonably priced, and they provided excellent support.

I was so mortified, so unconsolably miserable, that she finally but only partially relented. I was allowed to wear brown-leather penny loafers. They passed the "sturdiness" test, more or less.

I have finally forgiven my mother. I have also finally figured out her real motive for this uncharacteristically inflexible edict. The concern for my growing arches was a ruse. What really bugged her was the boring conventionality that pervaded both the Fifties and the instincts of adolescents. She'd have probably let me wear rubber flip-flops if I'd just thought of it myself — anything, but the same ol' black-suede penny loafers.

But it's the only time in all of my teen-age years I remember her being stuffy and stubborn, giving me the right message the wrong way. In fact, my teen years were better than most kids' because of my mom.

While other mothers were angered or terrorized by the moodiness, surliness or other horriblenesses of their teen-agers, mine relaxed. She thought my sister and I were fun and funny. She puttered around, comfortably drifting in and out of our activities, always encouraging, always positive.

When we lost sleep over our too-curly hair, she giggled. If we became hysterical about some thick-necked quarterback who never called, she hugged, sympathized and diverted. If we moaned about our awkward bodies, she praised and admired.

She thought we were wonderful and smart and we believed her. We still do.

It's been her best act, steering kids down the slippery slope of adolescence and onto the launch paid of adulthood.

She drew the line at some things, but it was a curving line, deftly making room for our unpredictable needs and natures. She brought sensitivity and good humor to the raising of teen-agers, and I hope I can, too.

Empathizing with the insecurity that blankets my teen, I try to find that curvy line between reinforcing what is special about him and helping him fit in. And let me wow you with my tolerance.

I have no problem with sloppy T-shirts, buzz hair cuts or most rap music. I don't even hyperventilate anymore when I see body piercings. But I draw the line at pumped-up, souped-up basketball shoes, worn with laces untied and costing more than the mayor makes in a month.

Besides, Mom's right. Everyone's wearing them.

EPILOGUE

My mother, Dorothy (Dottie) Mandell died in 1990. A fine musician and actor herself, I hate to think what she'd have thought of rap artists. Good natured and unconventional, open-minded and certainly no cultural elite, still, she had her standards. "What's with his miserable mouth?" she'd have probably said about Eminem. "Yuck! Who needs it?!" Who needs it, indeed.

A BIRTHDAY GIFT

DECEMBER 1994

You can do a lot when you're 18. Even legally. Maybe not wisely, but at least legally.

You can eat too many quarter-pounders with cheese, drive around in a gyrating car that sounds like a base woofer on wheels, have sex and use contraceptives (hopefully) without your parents even knowing, wear a baseball cap forward, backward or any which way you want.

You can watch lots of ESPN, play real sports or dress in camouflage and shoot at other people with paint guns; you can make the honor roll or blow off studying; burn CDs or burn rubber; get a job, lose a job, go to college, stay home.

You can be tried in a court of law as an adult. (You already have that honor in Oklahoma when you're only 13 and the charge is murder.) You can enter into some legal contracts and you can even get married. You can — must, in fact — register for the draft, and you can die for your country.

At 18 in America, you have reached your "majority," a term, according to Black's Law Dictionary, that means "full age; legal age, the age at which, by law, a person is entitled to the management of his own affairs . . ." or hers, I hope. Dear Mr. Black probably just didn't know any women of majority.

My son is 18 this week.

Now he is, legally and officially, entitled to manage his own affairs and to enjoy his civic rights, assuming there are any left for him to enjoy after the Republicans have a go at it.

I told him I was taking him out for a little birthday surprise on his lunch break. I know he was hoping to test drive a new Beamer or fit bindings on new skiis, but when he figured out we were headed for the nearest agency to register him to vote, he looked at me and smiled.

He knows I see this as a gift; indeed, a very valuable gift. If not a gift, it is a privilege afforded too few people in the world and not used by nearly enough of those who have it.

The right to vote doesn't come in the bottom of a crackerjack box. It's part of the Constitution of the United States. Every man and woman who served in every war the United States has been in has liked the gift well enough to fight and sometimes die for it.

The right to vote was not automatically included in the Constitution for everyone. Blacks and former slaves couldn't vote until the ratification of the Fifteenth Amendment in 1870. Before 1920 it was just a guy thing: women weren't given the right to vote until the Nineteenth Amendment was ratified.

And prior to ratification of the Twenty-Sixth Amendment in 1971, these funky 18-year-olds with their joyous hearts, TV-minds and risky lifestyles couldn't vote, either. Now they can, but they don't. Forty percent fewer 18- to 24-year-olds voted in the last election[1] than the rest of those eligible, and the reasons, while not certain, can be pretty well guessed at.

Why bother? they ask. I may be responsible and use my vote, but elected officials are behaving less and less responsibly. Indeed, today's teen-ager has seen our government contribute little to progress for the good, seeing instead the growing cynicism of their parents and older adults about their own lives and the government's capacity to impact them.

He or she sees too much violence, too much fear, too much hatred, too much stress, too many options, too much television, too much self-seeking and too little generosity. She or he has probably had too

[1] This refers to the mid-term Congressional and gubernatorial elections of 1994. In the 2000 presidential elections, the rate of participation in this age group was even smaller.

little education — especially civic and community education — too little respect for public service, too little respect for and from adults.

The pull of cynicism is great, so you may think this is all a lot of stupid Sixties stuff about saving the world. It's not.

One vote can matter. King Charles I of England was beheaded after a vote of 68–67; the Alaska Purchase of 1867 was ratified by just one vote; and Adolph Hitler was elected leader of his party in 1923 by a margin of just one vote.

I'm not so naïve to think my one vote, or yours, will change the direction of our country. Nor am I so irresponsible to throw away my one vote, the gift won for me with the blood, sweat and tears of our forefathers.

At the conclusion of the Constitutional Convention, Benjamin Franklin was asked, "What have you wrought?"

He answered, " . . . a Republic, if you can keep it."

Democracy, dudes, is not a spectator sport. Your vote is your voice. Use it.

Register, vote and happy birthday.

EPILOGUE

In the 2000 presidential election, after protracted squabbling, vote recounting, lawsuits filed and finally the involvement of the U.S. Supreme Court, George W. Bush was declared the winner of Florida's electoral votes by winning only approximately 600 votes more than Democratic candidate Al Gore out of more than 100 million cast. If 600 votes can make the difference, it becomes easier to see that every vote does count. On the other hand, the legal and public relations battles for the decisive Florida vote — a not-so-pretty picture that went on for weeks after election day — might have been enough to turn off even the most patriotic voter. Let's hope not.

TWO

OK BY ME

THE TREE
JUNE 1997

here are almost no trees in downtown Oklahoma City. The earth in the central part of this state is a funny kind of dry red clay, and between the challenges of growing things in this soil and the bulldozers of urban renewal, most trees seem to have given up, the job of staying alive just too tough.

In fact, I think downtown Oklahoma City has looked for a long time like it, too, has just given up. It is not very big, not very busy and, truthfully, not very pretty. There are a few shops, even fewer restaurants but hardly any people walking the windy streets. There are quite a few office buildings, though, some very tall, strongly built and handsome.

The Alfred P. Murrah Federal Building was one of the largest and strongest of those, but it isn't there at all anymore, destroyed by a 5,600-pound fertilizer bomb left in a yellow Ryder truck parked on one of those quiet downtown streets.

We've been holding our breath here in Oklahoma City, while a jury considered whether Timothy McVeigh, an able-bodied, well-spoken young man armed with a quiet but deep fury against his government, planted that bomb. Now the verdict is in. McVeigh has been found guilty.

The verdict was anti-climatic at best. It won't bring back the 19 children and 149 adults killed that day. It won't make whole those severely injured and physically disabled by the blast. It doesn't answer the painful question, "Why?" still screaming in the hearts of mothers and fathers who lost their babies.

About 50 yards north of the spot where McVeigh left the bomb, an elm tree stands in the center of a parking lot. A stubborn thing, it's not very pretty or very straight or very tall. Known by people around here as the Survivor Tree, this scruffy thing was not even touched by the power of this bomb which destroyed buildings for blocks to the north, east and west of it.

Oddly, surprisingly, maybe even miraculously, the tree has held on to its little spot in this red earth, losing its leaves over the two winters since the bombing, then somehow finding the strength to grow again in the two springs that have followed.

People are drawn to this strong, bullheaded tee. Groups of children gather around it to sing. Churches, synagogues and mosques call people to worship there. Ribbons are tied around it. Prayers are said before it; water is poured on it; lucky pennies are placed in it, all in homage to its toughness, its willingness to stand there and not give up its life in the face of unimaginable horror.

Soon, McVeigh will be gone — in prison, at least, possibly put to death. But the families of those who died that day and those of us who have lived and cried with them, are still here. Some are battling to stay alive themselves, holding on to their spot of rocky, red earth, not giving up on life. All rebuilding their lives in their own ways.

And finally, our city is going to rebuild downtown — a new ballpark, music hall, sports center and library. And a memorial built to remember our dead, with the Survivor Tree playing a central part.

A few hours after the McVeigh verdict was announced, several hundred survivors of the bombing and family members of those killed gathered around the elm. They raised their voices, not in celebration or chant of retribution or even in religious song, but oddly, surprisingly, miraculously and with great dignity they sang, "God Bless America."

Struggling mightily to bear their grief, their song said they still loved this land.

Their song said that hope is brighter than despair, that love is stronger than death and that justice can overpower tyranny.

Their song said that, in spite of everything they have endured, they would survive beside this strong tree, on this spot of strong earth, in the center of a strong community, in the heart of the very nation their enemy would rage against.

EPILOGUE

In April 2000 a national memorial to the victims and survivors of the Murrah Federal Building bombing was dedicated on the former site of the building. Covering a full city block, the memorial includes a 70-foot round elevated promontory that encircles the Survivor Tree. Inscribed on the outside of the promontory's wall a tribute to those who aided in rescue operations reads, "To the courageous and caring who responded from near and far, we offer our eternal gratitude."

On the inside of the wall, a second inscription reads, "The spirit of this city and this nation will not be defeated; our deeply rooted faith sustains us."

In the years following the bombing, the tree has grown stronger, taller and fuller, its branches reaching higher into the Oklahoma sky.

SELF-APPOINTED CENSORS
APRIL 1997

For months, Oklahoma City's Metropolitan Library System has drawn the ire of a local group called Oklahomans for Children and Families.

OCAF objects to the library's open-access policy which insures free access to information by all citizens, regardless of age, a legal responsibility it has to the community under the First Amendment. But it is a policy which OCAF and its president Bob Anderson believe allows access to certain materials in the library they deem inappropriate for children.

OCAF objects, particularly, to three young adult fiction titles and two sex education books. They want these books, along with 100 or so others, kept in a closet away from children younger than 16.

I haven't read the books. My reading of young adult fiction runs more toward Mark Twain, whose known-to-be-tawdry "Adventures of Huckleberry Finn" was the target of other enlightened book banning efforts in 1996. As far as sex education goes, you bet there's more I'd like to know, but I ain't going to the library to get it.

OCAF says the books are dirty, so Oklahoma City Council member Frosty Peak proposed a resolution asking the library to "consider modifying existing policies or adopting new policies to provide for segregation of materials" that, among other things, "Contain ... descriptions of explicit sex or violence." The Village (a separate self-incorporated, city within the Oklahoma City limits) has essentially done the same thing; The Daily Oklahoman agrees, as does the local chapter of the Christian Coalition. I guess they all know dirty when they see it.

Peak and five other Council members, including , sadly, the mayor, voted for the successful resolution. They have apparently lost sight of the First Amendment and their duty to protect us from those who would stand in our way of honoring it. Who are these people, anyway, telling us what we or our children can or cannot read?

"By its very mission," wrote library system director Lee Brawner to Peak, "the ... system represents diversity, and its collection includes ideas and information that are both popular and accepted as well as ideas and information that are unpopular and controversial."

Brawner is not only right, he has shown extraordinary professionalism, patience and class in his handling of this matter. Acknowledging OCAF's right to object, the library has proposed a compromise — a parental preference option, which puts the decision for which books children may check out in the hands of parents where many believe it belongs, not in the hands of the library, the Council or OCAF.

But wait. If it's sex and violence we're rooting out, better lock those Bibles in that closet, too. Many stories hath been told there that would make Larry Flynt blush.

In Genesis, Chapter 38, for example, when marriages were pre-arranged, Judah found a wife, Tamar, for Er, his first-born son. But Er was wicked "and the Lord slew him." So, as was the custom, Judah ordered his second son, Onan, to "come in unto" Tamar and keep the lineage going. But Onan only liked the coming in unto her part, so just as he was finishing up, he withdrew, allowing "his seed to spill onto the ground," lest his brother get the credit. God slew him, too.

Then Judah (giving new meaning to the word patriarch) told Tamar to go home and wait 'til his third son was old enough to come in unto her. Home she went.

In the meantime, Judah's wife died. While looking for company, Judah happened onto Tamar, who by this time had either disguised herself as a prostitute or had to live like one after being passed around by Judah's boys.

After paying her off with a few goats, Judah also came in unto Tamar and then, to complicate matters, Tamar conceived, and when Judah found out, he was fit to be tied. He ordered her burned, but then changed his mind and she had twins.

Not to mention Chapter 34's Dinah, raped by a Canaanite big shot, then avenged by her 12 brothers who tricked the Canaanite men by promising them the rest of their women and a bunch of cows and donkeys if they'd agree to be circumcised. While the guys were holding their asses in post-op, the bros murdered them all in retribution.

Now there are some wholesome stories for pre-schoolers, eh, Mr. Anderson?

EPILOGUE

Oklahomans for Children and Family also brought Oklahoma City one of its most infamous and embarrassing moments in 1997.

Hearing an alarming report on a Christian radio program about "an obscene movie," OCAF leader Anderson sent a few of his foot soldiers down to the local Blockbuster video store and a branch of the county library to nab the Oscar-winning foreign film "The Tin Drum."

Based on his book of the same name, Gunter Grass' film is the surreal story of one German boy's protest of the Nazis, a protest he makes by refusing to grow up. In one dream-like scene, the adolescent boy and a young girl appear unclothed and sexually engaged.

Indeed, the OCAFers were horrified. They gave it to the Oklahoma City Police – who had actually sent an officer to the OCAF office. The police took it to a state district judge who advised them it was child pornography.

The police then confiscated all known copies from the library, the video store and the private individuals who had rented them. The police learned who rented the movie after scaring video store clerks into believing they had to give over that information. Then they banged on people's doors and demanded they give up their copies.

Michael Camfield, development director for the Oklahoma affiliate of the ACLU and one of the individuals who rented the video, subse-

quently sued the city, the district attorney and several individual police officers, alleging violations of his First Amendment rights, the right to due process, Fourth Amendment search and seizure rules and violation of the Video Privacy Protection Act of 1988. The U.S. District Court for the Western District of Oklahoma ruled that the film was legal under Oklahoma state law and could be returned to library and video store shelves.

In addition, the National Video Software Dealers Association and the National Association of Recording Merchandisers sued the parties involved, primarily the City of Oklahoma City, and settled out of court, opting not to pursue the Fourth Amendment search and seizure issue. Those groups received $400,000 in attorneys fees from Oklahoma City and $175,00 from the Oklahoma County district attorney.

Until all the litigation has been settled, the financial costs to the city and county are unknown, but they are already upward of $500,000 and could go higher.

The episode was reported by many national news outlets – in print and broadcast – and was generally treated with a snicker across the country. Since then, OCAF has primarily confined its activities to a quieter role as on-line monitor of pornography sightings.

GAYLORD FAMILY VALUES
JANUARY 1999

Last week, the Columbia Journalism Review added its hefty weight to the now-national conversation about The Daily Oklahoman, Oklahoma City's only full-news daily and the largest paper in the state, published by the Oklahoma Publishing Co. (OPUBCO). Among other things, CJR calls the Oklahoman "a fat, incurious monopoly."

In an article titled, "The Worst Newspaper in America," CJR writer Bruce Selcraig added his remarks to those of James Risser published in the June 1998 issue of the American Journalism Review. CJR is the 38-year-old, bi-monthly journal of the Columbia University Graduate School of Journalism that examines the performance of journalists and journalistic publications.

Selcraig's piece confirms what most of us already know and dislike about the stubborn, scolding Oklahoman. Apparently, attempts to reach publisher E.L. Gaylord for the story didn't produce much. Gaylord told the reporter to "Go on home" and hung up on him.

But CJR's own presupposing reporting doesn't tell us what to do about our state's biggest daily, and it gives those at the paper with an already bunker-like mentality an excuse to dismiss valid criticism as unfounded. Well-researched and snappily written, the CJR piece minces no words.

- "Want lots of enterprising, in-depth stories with plenty of world and national news in your newspaper's front section? How about praline recipes instead?"
- "Reporters cringe when they have to attach their bylines to F.O.D.s ('front office deals') — comically inflated stories involving Gaylord's business, religious or social interests."

- " . . . filler and flotsam crowds out a remarkable amount of real news."

Most of the criticism in this article was mentioned by AJR (few minorities on staff, unimaginative writing, editorial opinions grounded far to the right of mainstream, no opposing views, outdated graphics, always partisan, etc.), but a few practices at the paper were particularly disturbing.

Selcraig wrote about two-time U.S. House candidate Paul Barby, who is gay. A 63-year-old rancher from Western Oklahoma, Barby went to the Oklahoman with a lesbian activist to talk to editorial writer J.E. McReynolds about the "hateful tone" of a particular editorial.

After a brief hello in a conference room, Barby said, McReynolds excused himself and returned with two members of First Stone Ministries, an Oklahoma-based group that wants to save homosexuals by converting them to heterosexuals.

" 'I'd like you to talk with these people,' Barby quotes McReynolds as saying. 'I'll just listen.' "

"Where else can you find a big-city editorial page . . . obsessed with lecturing gays?" wrote Selcraig.

And then there are the Oklahoman's advertising rates: A full-page, one-time, black-and-white ad costs about $145.00[1] per thousand of circulation compared to about $80 in the nearby Dallas Morning News. This is particularly galling from a newspaper in a state whose per capital income hovers at around 80 percent of the national average.

But the CJR piece is not altogether fair itself. While quoting some objective outside sources, most of the former Oklahoman staffers quoted left the paper with ill feelings and probably have axes to grind.

---

[1] In spring, 2001, the Daily Oklahoman's approximated rate is $189.00 per thousand; the Dallas Morning News is $102.00 per thousand.

CJR could have let us in on both sides of those stories, or found staff members who left on principle.

Nor does CJR mention the Oklahoman's more recent and very aggressive investigative series on the alleged improprieties of former state Insurance Commissioner John Crawford, a Republican. Previously, Republican politicians and elected officials could expect OPUBCO to turn a deaf ear to suggestions of corruption.

Also, former Gov. David Walters, Democrat, told the writer he felt he was the target of relentlessly critical coverage during the period he was under investigation for violating campaign finance laws. But any paper worth the newsprint it's printed on would cover, vigorously, a governor under criminal investigation who ultimately pleaded guilty to violating the law.

And last week, I noticed the Oklahoman ran a piece about sex education, naming the once-despised Planned Parenthood organization as a source for such information.

As in the earlier AJR piece, CJR finds some good things about the Oklahoman, such as likeable editor Ed Kelley; "some fine reporting last year on pollution from corporate hog farms;" staff members who say they enjoy working there; and an occasional courageous story — though none were cited in the last 20 years.

The story also lauds the paper's first publisher, Edward K. Gaylord.

"Although a strident opponent of unions, welfare and socialists, Gaylord vowed that his newspaper would never become 'offensively' partisan,' " Selcraig wrote.

" 'We shall strive [E.K. Gaylord] wrote in a 1916 editorial,' " 'to be a people's paper in the best sense of the term.'"

Now, two national journals concur that today's publisher, Edward L. Gaylord, seems not to share these admirable goals. Hello there, OPUBCO? Anyone listening?

Many of us who live here and read, or refuse to read, the Oklahoman wonder if the paper actually reflects the values of our community or if those values have been created by, as Selcraig calls him, "one grumpy publisher."

EPILOGUE

After these two national journals blasted the paper, someone at OPUBCO took notice. Editor Kelley took himself to the national bureau in Washington, D.C., and OPUBCO hired a new editor. Stan Tiner, a seasoned, moderate-to-conservative editor from Alabama, was a registered Democrat, but he was a newspaperman first and a partisan second. He rode into town and immediately shook things up at the paper, launching a much more aggressive approach to investigative reporting, changing the look of the paper and shaking things up internally.

Conversations around town about investigative stories in the paper were lively. A local police scandal was well reported and hotly debated, resulting in serious and helpful changes in police procedure. Environmental stories exposed sacred corporate cows, fairly and accurately, but with a toughness never before read in the paper. You could tell the new editor was making a difference, that writers were working harder and readers were optimistic about the new direction at the daily.

But apparently somebody upstairs at the paper wasn't very happy with Tiner or all of the changes or both, and he was gone within months. Since then, the paper is back to presenting pabulum.

The Daily Oklahoman's power in this community is enormous, setting the tone for other media in Oklahoma City for so long, everyone else – especially in television and radio – have gotten lazy, I guess.

There's nothing inherently wrong with folksy, which is the Oklahoman's style. But in an era when the world is moving at warp speed and news about technology and change is available online, on cable and in an ever-increasing number of aggressive publications, print journalism, especially newspapers, needs to keep up or get out of the way. Today journalists write thoroughly, provocatively and energetically for readers who want ever-more information and want it now. They can get it, too, so folksy and small-town becomes just too slow and inadequate.

I do believe that an informed, well-read populace, encouraged to ask questions and debate issues makes for a healthy, prosperous community. But this paper has kept this town down for so long it must look like up by now.

The paper remains an insult and an embarrassment and, I believe, one of the reasons this city is not taken seriously outside the state. Instead of taking any of this criticism to heart, these jibes have only deepened the paper's resolve to maintaining its stubborn status quo.

Maybe with new, younger leadership from the Gaylord family, OPUBCO will arrive in the 21st Century. Maybe the publishers can see a role for themselves as aiding progress and listening to citizens rather than dictating values and parceling out information. I do believe that if the paper doesn't change, and soon, the town won't, either.

HEAT

AUGUST 1990

Heat . . . sizzling heat . . . Promethean heat . . . prickly heat . . . blinding heat . . . The Long Hot Summer. "We're having a heat wave, a tropical heat wave . . . " disco inferno, Burn Baby Burn . . . too hot to handle . . . Pease-porridge hot . . . hot and bothered . . . hot tamale . . . hot potato . . . hot dog . . . hot tempered . . . hot headed.

"It's too hot, too hot baby, better run for shelter, better run for shade" . . . if you can't stand the heat, get out of the kitchen.

"Here comes the sun, little darling" . . . Don't just stand there and let the sun burn a hole in ya . . . In the Heat of the Night . . . like a raisin in the sun . . . "For he shall be like the heat in the desert, and shall not see when good cometh."

Some Like it Hot . . . Good Day Sunshine . . . "Come on, baby, light my fire" . . . There'll be a hot time in the old town tonight . . . in the house of the rising sun . . . red hot 'n' blue . . . hotsy-totsy . . . hotcakes . . . hot diggity dog . . . "Surprised was I with sudden heat which made my heart glow" . . . "Sunshine came softly through my window today . . . "

"You are my sunshine, my only sunshine, you make me happy when skies are gray."

"Not snow, no, or rain, nor heat, nor night keeps them from accomplishing their appointed courses with all speed" . . . The queen of hearts she made some tarts, all on a summer's day.

"Shall I compare thee to a summer's day?" But it's too darned hot . . . Mad dogs and Englishmen go out to the midday sun . . . "hot town summer in the city, back 'o my neck gettin' dirty and gritty" . . . "moral equivalent of war; analogous, as one might say, to the mechanical equivalent of heat."

"Goodness, gracious, great balls of fire!" . . . The Towering Inferno

...and in the metro area, sunny and hot again today... "and they whose hearts are dry as summer dust burn to the socket" ... "one draught above heat makes him a fool, the second mads him and a third drowns him" ... "Double, double, toil and trouble, fire burn and cauldron bubble" ... up in smoke ... "We didn't start the fire; it was always burnin' since the world's been turnin'."

"Heat cannot of itself pass from a colder to a hotter body" ... just add hot water and serve.

"... or art thou a dagger of the mind, a false creation proceeding from the heat-oppressed brain."

OUR TOWN
APRIL 1995

PROLOGUE

A few minutes before 9 a.m. on April 19, 1995, Timothy McVeigh, a young man with a deep and burning hatred for the U.S. government, drove a rented, yellow Ryder truck east on N.W. 5th Street in downtown Oklahoma City. He parked the truck in front of the main entrance to the nine-story Alfred P. Murrah Federal Building, got out and left the truck.

At 9:02 a.m., a 5,600-pound fertilizer and fuel bomb, placed in the back of the truck by McVeigh, exploded as intended, demolishing the front half of the office building from the ground up. After days of clearing away the rubble and debris and rescuing those who survived, the death toll reached 168, including 19 children.

The bomb went off just as people were settling into their desks in the federal building and just as parents were taking their infants and children into the day care center on the first floor of the building.

The building housed offices for a long list of federal agencies, including the Social Security Administration; the Bureau of Alcohol, Tobacco and Firearms; the Secret Service; Immigration and Naturalization; the U.S. Department of Agriculture; and U.S. Department of Housing and Urban Development.

Hundreds of doctors, nurses and rescue personnel began immediately setting up triage and care units on site which funneled the injured into other medical settings at area hospitals.

Fire fighters and police – from Oklahoma City, surrounding towns and even from states beyond Oklahoma – sprang into action, digging for injured victims, clearing debris, pulling bodies from the wreckage. The recovery effort continued into the following month as the final three bodies were pulled from the rubble.

Religious groups established shelters throughout the city for refuge, both physical and spiritual. Social workers, psychologists, psychiatrists and counselors spread out between various sites established to comfort victims and their families. Food banks made supplies available to rescue workers; the American Red Cross began its highest level of relief aid; money poured in from individuals and organizations wanting to help; and from all parts of the city and state, individuals arrived in downtown Oklahoma City, lining up to help.

McVeigh was picked up on an unrelated offense, just hours after the bombing, near the small town of Perry, Okla.

That same year, a federal grand jury indicted McVeigh and his friend, Terry Nichols, for murder and for the bombing conspiracy. The pair were prosecuted in federal court in Denver for the murders of the eight federal law enforcement officers who died in the explosion.

McVeigh was convicted and sentenced to death. Nichols, who helped mix the bomb and finance the bombing, was convicted of involuntary manslaughter and given a sentence of life in prison. At both trials, federal prosecutors were aided by the testimony of Michael Fortier, a one-time friend of McVeigh's.

Prosecutors were able to prove the pair were motivated, in part, by the fiery end to a standoff between U.S. law enforcement officials and the residents of the Branch Davidian Compound in Waco, Texas, that occurred on the same day, April 19, in 1993.

 The land is flat here — flat, red and hard like the rusty-colored granite that was, until last week, the composition of the Alfred P. Murrah Federal Building in the middle of downtown Oklahoma City.

It's so flat that from some vantage points far away, you can even see the building which now looks as if someone reached down with a jagged pruning hook and gouged out the center. This building was, until last week, the workplace of about 500 government employees and a safe haven for 30 children sheltered in an on-site day care center.

It's so flat and dry and dusty here you worry that maybe this eroded red earth, this endless gritty wind and this dry, dry land has made all of us who live here hard and dry and brittle, too. Daily, you steel yourself to the wind and the dust; you try to appreciate the pace of an easy, every-day life where nothing fantastic ever happens, but nothing very terrible happens either.

You accept that our city will never host the Olympics. You know Broadway producers won't suddenly bring great theater here. You know Michael Jordan or Nolan Ryan will never play here, that you won't see Hollywood stars eating at fabulous restaurants or world leaders arriving for a summit.

If something really significant did happen here, you wonder, would we be hard and dry and dusty in its face, too?

But those were yesterday's questions, before my children heard and felt an explosion sitting in their classrooms four miles away from downtown, before my husband and his co-workers felt their 33-story building convulse, before hundreds of people — too many of them babies and young children — would be counted as dead, buried beneath that dry granite. Now all that hardness has turned to dust, and hundreds more people roam the streets, hospitals and make-shift shelters desperate to find family or friends on a list of "treated and released."

Since I have lived here, I have been afraid that this land and its dull, near-barren character had eroded our energy, our ambition and our spirit. But that was yesterday, before our under-funded, previously criticized police department responded with speed, efficiency and calm. That was before thousands of people lined the streets to give blood within just two hours of the explosion.

That was before hundreds of doctors, nurses and medical personnel came, unbidden, from towns like Waurika, Seminole, Tulsa, Shawnee and Choctaw to lend a hand. That was before our fire department launched a rescue effort far beyond anything they had done before and far beyond anything many cities could handle at all.

Within a few hours of the bomb's explosion, we had more volunteers, more donations of food, water, blankets, medical equipment and counseling than we needed.

We had a city-wide media effort that delivered fast, accurate and helpful information – unsensationalized and trustworthy. We had elected officials who, a week before, were sniping at each other over nothing, now standing arm-in-arm giving us reasons for optimism. We had a system of hospitals, doctors and nurses so generous and competent there was, quite literally, one doctor available for every single patient brought to them.

Here is what I have learned this week about the people who live simply and quietly in Oklahoma City. We are responding, not only to the worst act of terrorism to occur in the United States, but to events of much greater significance – one man's life, one woman's mother, one neighbor's friend; each person's toil, each family's bond, each child's future.

A SEAL FOR ALL OF US

OCTOBER 1995

PROLOGUE

The Christian cross formerly occupied one quadrant of the official seal of Edmond, Okla., a suburban city to the north of Oklahoma City. After a three-member panel of the U.S. Court of Appeals for the 10th Judicial Circuit determined that the cross was an endorsement of religion by the city and should be removed, the city of Edmond did that, leaving the quadrant blank. The city then appealed this decision to the U.S. Supreme Court in 1996, but the Court declined to hear the case, letting the decision of the lower court stand.

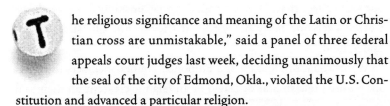 he religious significance and meaning of the Latin or Christian cross are unmistakable," said a panel of three federal appeals court judges last week, deciding unanimously that the seal of the city of Edmond, Okla., violated the U.S. Constitution and advanced a particular religion.

The decision stunned many Edmond residents: "It's a bunch of hooey!" cried one for whom Christianity is a fact of life. For them, the members of this majority religion, there was no problem. On Sundays all the churches are full, said one fellow. But for those of us for whom Christianity is not a fact of our lives, the seal was an uncomfortable reminder that, in fact, we are not part of the official community.

Of course the cross is a religious symbol. Everyone with two eyes — including the Islamic, Hindu, Jewish, Buddhist and other varied citizens of Edmond — knows it to be the strongest, clearest symbol of Christianity. Besides, there are lots of reminders.

Every time I open a letter from the City of Oklahoma City, I find myself asking, "Is this my city, too?" (The invitation to the Christian

Businessman's Prayer Breakfast really throws me, since I'm neither of those things.)

By the looks of the city's official letterhead, police cars, insignias on uniforms or pin given to me for service on a city commission, Oklahoma City is a Christian city. The cross on our city's seal, as sure as the cross on the official seals of Edmond, The Village and apparently many other towns in the state, says so. There never has been any pretense about it.

I didn't find the court's decision "preposterous," then, as Edmond's Mayor Bob Rudkin did. Edmond's official emblem bearing the cross is an announcement for all the world that Edmond is a religious community, specifically a Christian religious community. No pretense. No fooling anybody. No bones about it.

A little myopic maybe ("Since most of us are Christians, shouldn't our seal reflect that?"). A little insensitive, possibly ("We've always treated everyone fairly here; even if they're not Christian, they'll understand.").

What would Mr. Rudkin and Edmond's council members think of a six-pointed Jewish Star of David or an Islamic crescent on their seal, their police cars, their stationery, their uniforms? Some years ago, when Moslem members of the Edmond community wanted to build a mosque there alongside Christian churches, a great uproar ensued. The mosque was eventually built, but the Moslems in Edmond were certainly reminded that their town was dominated by a Christian majority.

It could be argued that defending this symbol on the seal was a little foolhardy, too. The legal precedent for this decision was so strong, it's hard for Edmond's leaders to justify the $74,000 they spent in taxpayer money to hire an outside attorney to fight this case. A friend, not coincidentally a resident of Edmond, points out that for the approximately 61,000 residents of that town, the lawyer's bill cost each and every one of them more than $1 — Christian and non-Christian alike.

Surely they will not waste any more of their citizens' money trying to convince the U.S. Supreme Court to hear a case like several others it has already turned down.

Mr. Rudkin finds this decision preposterous. He feels there's "a concerted effort to remove all semblance of religion from public life."

There's not. There's just a concerted, time-honored, revolution-tested, constitutionally guaranteed right to remove one group's religion from official public life over any one else's. I hope Oklahoma City will follow the wisdom of the 10th judicial circuit and remove the cross from our seal, too.

Many of us who live, work, study, do business, volunteer and contribute to this city are not Christians. We do these things not because we're Christians or Jews or belong to any particular religion, but because we're neighbors. Without a cross on the seal, the neighborhood would include us all — officially.

EPILOGUE

The City of Oklahoma City has a Christian cross on its seal, as well, but hasn't removed it or been told to by any legal authority. As of February 2001, the City of Edmond had removed its original seal from most places it had appeared. The seal still appears on the flag at City Hall and depicts several other images — a landmark building on a college campus, a wagon from the days of the Oklahoma Land Run, some oil rigs and one blank, white space. The drawing of the cross never has been replaced with anything, and city attorneys tell me the old seal is no longer in use. I guess if Edmond can't say publicly that it's Christian, it won't say anything at all.

THE CITY'S BEST

AUGUST 1993

ust when August's dog days hang over our city like a wet heat pack, we at the Oklahoma Gazette dare to pull you out of your doldrums with our annual Best of Oklahoma City issue.

Come in out of the sun, put your feet up, grab a beer and remind yourself of the best our city has to offer.

I escaped the heat this summer, and have been away from Oklahoma City. But great distance brings great perspective, and from afar I see some things about our town I've taken for granted when I'm up close and personal.

Like the air. You can breathe here. The Oklahoma air is beautifully clear and clean almost every day of the year. City government's air pollution measurers may disagree, but in most big-sized American cities, you look up and see brown or gray or creepy purple haze. Air is not supposed to be another thing to look at, but rather, something to look through.

Here, we can see the famous Oklahoma sky and lots of it. Soft pastel blues, pinks and golds in the summer; perfect robin's egg blues in the fall and silver-sliced pewter, gray and green-black in the dramatic storm seasons. We probably have that pesky, ever-present wind to thank for these clear vistas, but there's so little clarity in the rest of life, at least we can take a deep breath here, look up and see clear into the sky.

From wide open sky, it's a logical leap to think about our wide-open society. There are a few pockets of silly elitism, where a Rolex or a Jaguar or a lifetime membership in legacy-laden ladies leagues are prerequisites to being "in."

But there's precious little pretense. Enough frontier spirit still blows across our red dirt to welcome anyone with an idea and the energy to make it happen. You don't need fancy pedigrees or lineage here to build strong, healthy neighborhoods, a thriving community of artists, a core of committed volunteer activists and some world-class athletes.

True, it's hard to understand why we can't bring that same can-do spirit to making our schools safe and productive havens for learning, or filling our woefully hollow downtown storefronts or tackling growing violent crime or countering our limiting, negative, debilitating local media. We don't have it all, but we do have a lot.

Don't forget Will Rogers World Airport, another of our city's pluses. Did you ever try to pick up visitors in L.A. or New York? Set aside the entire day, including a trip to the pharmacy, first, for sedatives. Our airport is quick, uncrowded, well-planned and accessible. Easy to get in to the city and easy to spirit away.

Important, too, because without some distance and perspective often gained only after you've been far away, we forget what's best about living in Oklahoma City.

A GESTURE OF RESPECT
MAY 1990

I once lived in a big, crowded city where you only stopped your car for red lights and, in some neighborhoods, not even then. Getting where I had to go, on my time and my terms, was all that mattered once I slid behind the wheel of my car and bowed my neck for the self-absorbed journey across town going about my own business.

Occasionally, in the noisy chaos of the city, you'd see a hearse and some headlit cars in funeral procession. If it even occurred to you to stop, you'd dismiss it as unnecessary, unimportant and definitely unsafe. There was no police escort, certainly not a vital use of scarce city funds. So you'd grumble, "Someone's funeral," and impatiently look for a way to dart around the procession, lest you be delayed even two more minutes.

But people in Oklahoma stop their cars when a funeral procession passes. It was one of the first things I noticed here. There was time and space, and police help, to interrupt your own journey and acknowledge someone else's.

We have all been, or will be, in one of those cars in one of those processions. Moving through traffic beside friends and relatives who share your sadness, you look out of the shaded car window and watch life go on around you.

"Look at them," you find yourself thinking.

"To them, this is just a normal street, a normal route on their way to a normal, everyday kind of task. But for us in this car, on this street, this whole world seems to have stopped.

"Today our route is different from what it's ever been before. Can't they see that? How can everyone go on about his business when the business of our lives has stopped, nothing short of dead in its tracks?

"How can others go to restaurants for chatty, casual lunches when we are filing into the funeral home? How can they carry briefcases and grocery bags while we are carrying a casket? Is this loss ours alone? Are we so uniquely struck by this sorrow that our lives are the only lives called to a halt today?"

The business of living life does and should go on around, before, during and after a death. Nor do we expect or even want total strangers intimately involved in our grief.

But it is remarkably comforting to drive past delivery trucks, station wagons, pickups and sports cars, all of whose drivers have pulled over and stopped, managing to put a halt, too, to their busy lives just long enough to acknowledge some connection to our sadness and say, "We all know, or will eventually, just how you must feel."

THREE

FAMILY MATTERS

LOSING BUNNY
MAY 1996

sparkling, sunny spring weekend in the East, the snow had finally melted, and we were en route to a family weekend at our son's college. We piled our baggage and ourselves into a rental car at Boston's big, chaotic Logan Airport and headed south.

As we left the parking lot, our 12-year-old daughter cried out from the back seat.

"Oh, no," she moaned. "I left Bunny on the plane."

Bunny. A stuffed white rabbit more gray now than white, more unstuffed than stuffed.

Bunny. Last seen with pink ears wearing white cotton undies. The underpants weren't originally Bunny's, but he — or she; none of us has known for sure about Bunny's sexual orientation nor cared — was embarrassed by a bare behind, so Bunny was always properly covered with some borrowed skivvies.

Bunny. Who slept with her, snuggled with her, comforted and loved her and went everywhere with her since she was a toddler. Bunny. Now missing, probably gone. Fighting back tears, she struggled mightily to cope with what was for her a significant loss.

The next day would be her 13th birthday.

The next week she would begin to view her parents — the same parents who had always been her consolation, her support, her heroes — with annoyance, impatience and disdain for their astounding stupidity.

The next month she would become a "Bat Mitzvah," meaning a "daughter and keeper of the commandments" in a Jewish coming-of-age ceremony. Beginning with this ritual, she is expected and privileged to accept the adult responsibilities of her family's faith and community.

She looked at me soulfully, with the sad, wide blue eyes of my baby and the strong, wiser eyes of my soon-to-be young woman. I saw both of her sitting there in the back of the car, seat belt securely fastened.

Bunny was gone. The transition from childhood to womanhood had officially begun.

While boys have become "Bar Mitzvah" ("Sons of the commandment") since the sixth century C.E., the ceremony was not held for girls until 1922 when a rabbi introduced it to his congregation in New York for his own daughter. Now girls, too, are called before their congregations to participate in the Sabbath service and read from the Torah, the first five books of Moses. At last, a girl's transition from childhood to womanhood is honored in Judaism, too.

This girl has approached this occasion as she does most things, with determination, focus and street-smart good sense. She has found the daunting task of learning the language, values and rituals of her ancestors interesting. She has managed the typical teenager's balancing act — schoolwork, Hebrew school, daily pre-dawn training as a competitive figure skater, softball and, of course, a "heavy social life" — as a cheerful challenge.

It's hard work, but the harder the work, the better she likes it. Childhood and girlhood have been pretty smooth sailing for this girl.

But now, things could get more complicated. Soon she will begin choosing and preparing for her own life's work. Soon her street smarts will be tested, on and off the streets.

Almost as if to signal her entrance to young adulthood, Bunny disappeared. And with him innocence, simplicity and perfect love.

Bunny, asking for nothing, giving everything.

Bunny and his perfect love will be replaced with real love. This is how life works. Soon, there will be other loves and other losses — a friend, a boy, a man, a family. All most difficult, some more painful. No one can give or get perfect love.

" 'Real isn't how you are made,' " said the Skin Horse to the rabbit in the Margery Williams children's classic, "The Velveteen Rabbit."

" 'It's a thing that happens to you. When a child loves you for a long, long, time, not just to play with, but REALLY loves you, then you become Real.' "

" 'Does it hurt?' " asked the Rabbit."

" 'Sometimes,' " said the Skin Horse, "for he was always truthful."

" 'When you are Real you don't mind being hurt ... It doesn't happen all at once ... It takes a long time ... once you are Real, you can't become unreal again. It lasts for always.'"

Welcome to womanhood, my girl. Expect its losses, rejoice in its love.

A LIKELY STORY

SEPTEMBER 1993

There is a fine, exclusive private school in that bastion of tradition, Old Greenwich, Conn., that boasts George Herbert Walker Bush and a few Nobel laureates among its alumni.

Hanging just inside the entrance in plain view of the school's little uniformed 6- to 12-year-old elites-in-training is written the word "like" with a big circle drawn around it and the universally recognizable diagonal line slashing through its center.

No mistaking that message.

They've like had it with like in Connecticut. When the pitiful speech habits of a nation pervade even the mouths of these well-educated babes, things have gone too far.

Where did this come from, this maddening repetition of like? It like pops out all the time. It's not like it is occasionally misused by a few lazy teen-agers. It is used habitually, insidiously, sometimes subliminally and also every damn time you turn around.

From carpool lines to cocktail parties, otherwise articulate people suddenly begin throwing like in and around every sentence and every subject, almost like a mantra.

Is that it? Is it a mantra for the verbally challenged hyperspeakers among us? A word repeated so often, so resonantly it brings a kind of personal calm and centering to its user? Cozy and comforting? Is that why everyone is like saying like so often? I doubt it. Like just isn't like that.

Maybe it's a power trick from the One Minute Guide to Appearing in Charge Through Pop CultureSpeak. Lesson No. 1: Pause often and cunningly slide in a word like like that lets 'em know you're in the know. But no.

This little adjective/adverb/preposition/conjunction/noun or verb (it is handy) slips in and out of a phrase so fast you like barely notice it. Intimidating? More like seriously irritating.

Is it for emphasis? e.g: "He's like so hot and I was like oh, God, will he like ever talk to me?" Who? Who's like hot?

Perhaps the speaker is bending over backward to be politically correct. So that instead of, "She's driving like a woman," the more sensitive will use, "She's like driving like a woman." Still meant as an insult, to be sure, but now a watered down one.

Oh, where is Will Strunk when we need him? That pithy professor who, in 1919, penned a little book that was and is still the bible of English style and usage. "The Elements of Style" — later revised, but only slightly, by E.B. White — is still as concise as ever on the rules of writing and speaking English as clearly, cleanly and correctly as possible.

"It was a 43-page summation," said White about Strunk's original, "of the case for cleanliness, accuracy and brevity . . . 52 years later its vigor is unimpaired."

But could Strunk & White have foreseen the invasion of like? Could they have anticipated the extraordinary permeability of this hackneyed little four-letter word into the minds, term papers and speech patterns of our minds?

Like it's not like just the kids are doing it, although they are like really into it, but it's like everyone, everywhere.

Yes, Strunk & White did know. White, in his chapter called "Misused Words & Expressions," wrote, "Like. Not to be used for the conjunction 'as.' 'Like' governs nouns and pronouns. Before phrases and clauses, the equivalent word is 'as.'"

But the Messrs. of Style go on to tell us "the use of 'like' for 'as' has its defenders; they argue that any usage that achieves currency becomes valid automatically." Has like achieved currency? A nickel for every time my daughter and her teen-age gang use it, and I'd be like rich.

Yet Will & E.B. do recover.

"Like has long been widely misused by the illiterate," they write.

"Lately it has been taken up by the knowing and the well-informed, who find it catchy, or liberating and who use it as though they were slumming."

Catchy? Liberating? Do they like not see the magnitude of this? This like thing is like an epidemic, sweeping through schools like head lice, afflicting like even the self-styled, well-versed among us and like twisting our language and our tongues into like major knots of garble.

Give up like? Unlikely.

IRONMAN

OCTOBER 1987

At first I thought it was just bananas. The yellow kind. Without realizing it, I was buying dozens each week.

Then odd things began showing up in the pantry: boxes of a non-narcotic white powder, green and foul-tasting when mixed with water and subtly called Exceed. Next appeared hundreds of revolting whole-grain products, such as PowerBars, a form of flavored, compressed cardboard loaded with energy-inducers. And finally, in the garage, an Italian bicycle with French chains and a wheel without spokes.

What was going on?

My husband finally confessed — naturally after the plans were a *fait accompli* — he had submitted his name for entry in the Ironman contest, the ultimate triathlon held each year in Kona, Hawaii. This endurance test requires a 2.4-mile ocean swim (Yes, sharks have been spotted), a 112-mile bike ride and a 26.2-mile marathon run. And wouldn't you know it, they chose his name. Out of a jar. Some people have all the luck.

"You actually want to do this?" I asked incredulously.

"Oh, God!" worried his parents. "He's so thin!"

To describe this man as obsessive is to state the obvious. To describe me as frazzled and fragmented is also a given. All I know about working out is aerobic eating.

So you really had to be there to appreciate the negotiations over his six-month, five-hours-a-day training schedule. There was a lot of, "When this is over ..." and "Next year it's your turn, dear." After kicking and screaming (This technique does not work on obsessive types), I gave up and said, "Go and be well."

So off he went, biking, running and swimming all over this state and a few others to prepare for the ordeal. Some days he'd leave home on his bike at 6 a.m., returning late that afternoon from trekking to nearby towns like Luther, Okla., where his chief excitement was a chase from a stray pig or an admiring truck driver. He lived on Exceed, shredded wheat and determination. I lived on blind faith and diminishing patience and counted the days.

A week before the race, he left early for Hawaii to get used to the water and the terrain. Despite rumors, he did not swim over.

A week later, I arrived with our two kids, ages 10 and four, the day before the race. Immediately, we were swept up in the melee of 1,500 super-athletes and 4,000 awe-struck spectators watching and waiting.

Race day. 7 a.m. Into the Pacific waters they dove, bathed in the spectacularly beautiful sunrise over the Kona Coast, inspired by a display of Hawaiian hoopla and thrilled to be part of this exciting, nationally televised, world-class athletic event.

At each transition point, we caught a glimpse of our Ironman and cheered him on to the next event.

He raced out of the water and into his bike shoes and was off again. We three fans returned to the hotel, lunched, swam, napped and downed a few piña coladas in his honor. Six hours later, our triathlete tossed his bike and began the run, at 2:30 p.m. in the 90-degree-plus heat.

And then, way past sundown and 11 hours and 43 minutes after he began, he crossed the finish line.

To see it was to understand only part of the fantastic accomplishment it was. He beat his own "personal best." He finished in the top 35 percent, and even higher in his age group. His pride and happiness were mirrored by ours.

Finishing strong was a great feat, but the training was much of the accomplishment. Since May, he had biked more than 2,700 miles, run 650 miles and swam 218,000 yards.

An hour after the race, he wolfed down a cheeseburger, french fries, a Coke and apple pie. That might have been the best news of the day. Congratulations and welcome back, Ironman.

THE WHOLE CHILD

AUGUST 1996

t takes three alarm clocks, at least one parent — rapidly aging, I might add — and remarkable motivation for my 13-year-old daughter to drag herself out of bed at 4 a.m., five days a week.

She pulls on two pair of warm-up tights, a skimpy practice dress, a sweatshirt and wool gloves. She eats, loads water, snacks and stiff, expensive skates with sharp, expensive blades into a heavy bag and flies out the door in the dark to be driven to a skating rink way across town.

She skates two hours on weekday mornings before school and five hours on summer mornings. She competes three or four times a year in different cities. She's usually tired and sore. Some days are great: "I skated two clean programs during practice!" Some aren't: "I'll never get my double lutz, and I may kill myself trying." But she loves it, loves the hard work, the friendships, her coach, the music, the costumes. Most of all, she loves the satisfaction that comes from doing something difficult and doing it well.

The 1996 women's Olympic gymnastics competition and the accompanying publicity about injuries, young competitors, emotional and physical trauma and coaches who act like monsters was enough to give the parent of any athlete anxiety.

Watching American gymnast Kerri Strug fall, hurt herself badly, then get up and do it again all for "The Gold," was nearly unbearable. Yes, she was a brave little girl. But mostly, she is a little girl.

She would probably say she loves her sport, too. But do we see joy for the sport on these girls' faces, or everyone else's expectations — parents', coach's, friends'? How can a 13-year-old know what she wants from life or how much to sacrifice to get it?

Three doctors writing in the New England Journal of Medicine landed hard on organized gymnastics for the hardships it imposes on young girls. They list an alarming array of common physical injuries — stress fractures, delayed puberty, scoliosis, higher risk of osteoporosis and arthritis — and warn against emotional damage, as well. They find 62 percent of elite gymnasts have eating disorders, and depression is rampant among these girls who peak at 14, 15 or 16 and are left with damaged bodies, damaged psyches and little youth.

In a book, "Little Girls in Pretty Boxes: The Making and Breaking of Elite Gymnasts and Figure Skaters," the stories are even worse, portraying parents and their daughters as pawns in the hands of egomaniacal coaches. The book tells of anorexic girls, girls living and training in constant pain and suicidal girls.

So what to do about all this? Close down ice rinks that are springing up across the country to support this growing and popular sport? Return leotards and skates from thousands of little ones who start out having fun in gym class but may end up with shattered bodies and lives? Should we fire all the coaches?

None of this is possible or necessary. Not every gymnast or figure skater will get an elite ranking or go to the Olympics. But each of them can learn and grow and enjoy the unbeatable feeling of self-worth that comes from focusing energy and discipline on hard work without destroying body and soul in the process.

Another book about young girls, "Raising Ophelia," reports a different point of view. Girls involved in sports, it says, often find it easier to stay away from drugs, alcohol and tobacco. And they place much greater value on personal accomplishment than the empty status that comes from clothes or money or hanging with the "in" crowd.

The key to avoiding this obsession with making perfect athletes out of imperfect, growing children is us, their parents. Yes, the gymnastic and figure skating associations and the Olympic committees should impose rules that hold a coach's feet to the fire about training hours, injuries, competitors' ages, etc., as surely as they impose rules about how two feet must land on a mat for a "stuck" landing or how many revolutions make a medal-winning triple axel.

But parents are in charge of their children; coaches are only in charge of them as athletes. We cannot give over our children or our values to coaches or the pursuit of medals. Parents must work with coaches and athletic groups to insist on rest, nutrition, positive emotional support and encouragement for their kids. No parent or coach in their right mind should allow a child to pound on a vault horse or a cold, icy surface with a serious injury.

Training our children to be athletes is fine, but first we have to train them to respect their bodies and take care of themselves. The coach's job is to raise a child to be an athlete, respecting the whole child. A parent's job is to raise that whole child, training her to do her best to live a full, happy life — emotionally, intellectually, athletically.

ON THE WB

DECEMBER 1998

ulie is a young college student, like my daughter or yours. She meets Zach, a sweet considerate guy. He is crazy about her and, over many months, they become friends, soul mates and lovers. He may be the one.

One night, Julie and Zach begin to have sex. It's fine, but Julie does not want it to progress to intercourse and says no to Zach.

Stop, she says. Don't.

No, Zach. Stop! She says more forcefully.

But Zach doesn't stop. He forces himself on Julie, against all her protestations, even against her futile, now-panicked attempts to push him away.

She has no cuts, no bruises, no signs of assault, but she has been raped. Not by a masked intruder with a gun, not by someone she just met, but by someone she knows well, trusts and loves.

It came as a surprise to me to learn that this is how many rapes occur.

We think we know about rape: It's dark, you are attacked in your house, your car, on the street, maybe beaten, hopefully not killed, but viciously raped. We also know about date, or acquaintance rape, when a guy you have met or barely know forces you to have sex in spite of your objections.

But more likely, a woman, or a girl, is raped by someone like Zach. Someone she has known a while, someone she trusts and even loves. But someone who, one time, steps over the boundaries of what she, and presumably he, has set for herself and the relationship.

Zach didn't, or couldn't, hear Julie ask or tell him to stop. He turned a deaf ear and a lot of force to what she did and didn't want. Then, everything changed.

I learned about this common kind of rape at the most unlikely cultural outpost: Television. Not just the usual vapid, value-less, vast wasteland of television, but on "Felicity" on The WB.

The WB is a Warner Bros. television network, much of whose programming is heavily marketed to that vulnerable group of viewers, 14-to 20-year old girls. Programming for these teens usually is such tripe, it often adds to problems and pressures kids and their families are struggling to handle.

The WB's "Felicity" has been a welcome exception. Recently, the producers of this weekly show about college kids offered the Julie and Zach story in two parts, called "Drawing the Line," handling the problem of rape with more intelligence, sensitivity and value than I've ever seen on TV.

On "Felicity," Zach does indeed rape Julie. He just doesn't fully realize it. She's his girlfriend, after all, and she wanted to fool around, too. But after Zach forces Julie to go further than she wants, she is very shaken and left with feelings shared by many women who have been assaulted.

"I'll handle this," she tries to convince herself. Or more poignantly and typically, "It was my fault," she thinks. I led him on, I gave the wrong signals, I've had sex with other men, this is my problem.

Yet Julie knows that something went very wrong. She talks to her friend, Felicity, but mostly she withdraws into self-blame, depression and then troublesome anxiety. Luckily for Julie, her friends do something to help. They seek advice from one of the counselors at the college and learn the procedure, and the pitfalls, if Julie decides to report the episode.

The counselor is good news, especially from Hollywood. She is not moralistic, judgmental or a psychobabbler, but smart, sympathetic and above all, to the point – a rare television character. Julie's trust has been violated, she says. That's a serious problem for now and later, and she needs to talk about it.

Julie's friends finally prevail. They console and convince her that the assault was not her fault. They urge her to talk to someone, and she does.

Julie finally reports Zach's action, a hearing is held and he is asked to leave school. Next comes another surprise from Hollywood. Instead of Zach transforming into the villainous rapist we suspect he must be, he reminds us that between men and women, nothing is all good or all bad.

Instead of the anticipated anger from Zach, Julie and the viewer must contend with his genuine, true-to-character kindness and now, sadness. We see him realize, and even admit, that this is all his fault. He tells her how much he cares for her and knows that he has brought her great harm and destroyed their relationship, his college career and his own reputation. Now we're really confused, and paying attention, because this is certainly not your run-of-the-mill rapist.

Unwilling to oversimplify, "Felicity" again departs from Hollywood's usual pandering pulp. Julie neither forgives Zach, nor do either of them make any pretense about "getting back together." This is too serious; they won't get past it.

Indeed, rape is no lightly glossed-over matter. Saying, even meaning, you're sorry is not enough. It cannot happen again, and "Drawing the Line" actually gives teen-age viewers a way to understand why, as well as some ideas for dealing with it.

Date rape can be a hard call. But Julie knew, and so does anyone else forced into a sexual experience against his or her will.

Rape is rape. Assault is assault. No means no, not maybe, and stop means stop, even if you thought she wanted you to go on, even if he says he loves you. The WB got it right. Maybe with their help, our kids can, too.

TEETERING ACROSS A STAGE
MAY 1997

O n that star-studded evening when I accept my award for Best Mother in a Producing/Supporting/Directing/Editing role, I will certainly thank the following who have made my job easier:

- The designers of shoes for girls who, in a desperate reading of their profit and loss statements, dreamed up 6 x 3-inch cork heels with platforms for 15-year-olds.

- Hair colorists or pop artists or whoever the hell is making it possible for children to color (read: dye, paint, crayon, spray, glitter, dip) their hair any hue of black, purple, puce or whatever.

- The piercers among you offering any number of adorable accessories for plugging the holes you've already made (and charged for) in our children. Rings and studs for the ears, eyebrows, nose, navel. Bars for the tongue not, unfortunately, restraining bars on the tongue, just unbelievably ugly and painful ways to decorate that already too-busy body part.

- All of you fashion queens campaigning to educate children about unsafe sex while designing clothing that makes every unsure-of-herself 13-year-old girl an irresistibly seductive target in navel-bearing, cleavage-foisting T-shirts and shorts.

- You clever advertising execs who market this silly stuff in magazine and TV ads for girls younger than 17.

- And last but not least, all you super-smart script writers who include story lines about teachers seducing 16-year-olds; fathers seducing daughters and working girls comparing orgasms over expensive wines at dinner.

Thank you, thank you, all of you. Doing this job feels practically impossible most of the time, anyway. Thanks for raising the challenges while dramatically lowering the standards.

If my daughter and her pals are reading this — and because their media-savvy little brain cells are always scanning, you can be sure they are — they will no doubt roll their eyes and write me off with an annoyed, "Whatever."

But dork though I may be, I do get it. It's middle school graduation week for my daughter, a time of high excitement and high anxiety. As she looks back on 11 years in a school that has been the source of growth, security, intellectual and emotional challenges, she doesn't want to leave. Who can blame her? School will never again be so sweet and nurturing.

As the curtain opens on a new stage, high school, she may be excited and hopeful, but mostly she is scared. Scared because it isn't just her friend or her brother or the kids in her math class who will be doing this new thing, it is she — the center of attention, the one of whom there will be expectations and demands, the one who will matter the most. Even walking across the stage is scary.

How will I do it? She must be wondering. How will I stand all that focus on me, all those new and difficult things? How will I do this away from a place where I feel so safe and in a new place where I only feel — me?

"Me," of course, is the issue. She cannot know yet who she really is, but she is searching madly in every direction to find out, and the easiest place to start is on the outside. She wants to make this transition, to walk across that graduation stage looking as special and sure of herself as she knows she should be feeling. She wants special hair, a special dress, a special necklace and, naturally, special, very tall shoes, all sort-of-but-not-exactly like everyone else's. If it's too old or too tall or too risky for her, she wants them anyway. At least she will look the part, even though she may be feeling "whatever."

Every middle school mother I know this week is doing battle over platform shoes, hair color and low-cut dresses. But I think I'll stop. She will walk onto that transitional stage looking exactly like who she is; a girl becoming a young woman; a girl becoming herself in her sweet, delicate dress and clunky, tough-girl shoes.

She may not be so certain, but I am confident that all this apprehension and uncertainty teeters atop a sure and solid foundation we have all worked hard to build. Her balancing act has just begun.

FOUR

KITH 'N' KIN

STILL DEAD?

DECEMBER 1995

amily and folks. Our kin, our relatives, our gang. The bunch, the lot, the litter, the whole kit 'n' kaboodle. Thanksgiving, Chanukah, Christmas, whatever. 'Tis the season, and we're all at home for the holidays.

At my house, a well-lighted Menorah and gluttonous attacks on potato pancakes piled high with sour cream and apple sauce. Across the street, twinkling lights in every tree and gluttonous attacks on turkey and ham.

God, what sumptuous scenes of familial fun, brotherly love, sisterly serenity, children with their faces aglow and mother . . . uh, Mother? Where the hell is Mother?

I look around thinking she — the mother, the mom, la madre, the real star of these family holidays — is just about to waddle out of the bedroom, gray hair sleep-flattened against her head, huddled under her ancient chenille bathrobe — the old, worn kind with the fluffy cotton lumps all over it, not today's smooth, silky, expensive kind.

She is just turning around from her station in front of the oven, waving a spatula at me and giggling, "So? Don't just stand there! Get busy grating those potatoes."

She is wrapping my Chanukah gifts.

"Books, what else? Why not learn something, for a change, instead of just giving in to all those ridiculous fashion fads," she says.

She is arguing, and losing, with my dad.

"A Christmas tree? Are you crazy? Guess what? We're not Christians. We don't celebrate Christmas. OK, OK. At least hide it in the den, away from the front windows in case the rabbi drives past."

She has put off shopping too long, has dragged me along and now we are lost in a parking lot. She has no idea where her car is.

"You see?" she moans. "This is why I hate cars. This is why I hate malls. They're all alike, so confusing, so dangerous. Oh, there it is!"

"That one?" I shriek. "The one with the stupid plastic flower taped to the antenna? Oh, Mother, how embarrassing."

"We found the car, didn't we?"

My mother has been dead for six years, and I think it's time for her to stop.

Admittedly, this has been an interesting phase, this dead part, but enough is enough. We experienced a difficult but dignified death, a cathartic coping period, a normal grieving phase.

Then we had a lot of silence, during which time we heard not a word from you.

During this, the holiday season, I get occasional communiqués, mostly having to do with your unearthly observations that I am spoiling my children, cooking the latkes in too much fat and, as always, doing too much.

"My God! Don't you ever stop? Sit down, put your feet up, tell me EVERYthing."

Beginning about Year Five A.M. (After Mom) I actually wanted to tell her everything. Now I'll talk, I thought. But just show up, will ya? The novelty of this death-is-part-of-life stuff has worn off.

I'd love to know what you think about my new kitchen and my old husband. And how 'bout that Madeleine Albright — Wow! A woman Secretary of State!

Have you heard the debate about butter vs. margarine? Can you believe your grandson is six feet tall? Do you like my hair short or long? Any opinion about estrogen replacement therapy? And get a load of my daughter's retro fashion look. Oh, so excuse me. I forgot you turned your nose up at polyester in 1968, so you're probably asking, "What's to like now?"

Please bring the recipe for sweet potato casserole, including the cooking time. I burn it every year. Bring that long-running list of everything you've done since last we talked but forgot to mention to me and, oh yeah, bring some more books.

Also, I'd like to know where you've been the last six years. Did you finally get a good night's sleep? Can you still hear Daddy snoring? Do they put candles on the Menorah up there or still use that same old vessel of oil? Are we in trouble for having the tree in the den?

It's time to knock it off, Mother. We're all home for the holidays, and you're no where to be found. Just come on down, we always have plenty of food. Besides, I'd much rather see you at the holidays than when I look in the mirror.

THE MAESTRO
JUNE 1999

My father is a musician of sorts.

Not to mislead you, he doesn't sing or play an instrument. He doesn't compose or conduct music. He can't even whistle very well. But he does make music.

On a wall in his home in Dallas a brass plaque reads, "Bud's Conservatory," and just beyond the plaque a door opens into a closet.

It's a small closet, stacked ceiling to floor with stereo and recording equipment, CDs, records, cassette tapes and labels. Just a closet to most of us, but a world of pleasure to my dad, Bud.

In this spot, Bud makes music. For over 85-plus years of life, he has channeled his enjoyment of music into this mini recording-studio-in-a-closet. In the Conservatory (hah!) he plays CDs for hours, listening to sounds old and new, operatic and swing, vocalists and soft jazz, Broadway and boogie.

His own collection is enormous, but listening is not all he does. From his ever-growing collection, he selects tunes and numbers that describe an era or capture a particular artist or simply reflect what he likes. Then he compiles his selections, records them on audio cassettes — complete with informative and historical commentary by, of course, Bud himself — and mails them to family and friends.

At first he made tapes just for my sister and me. Now he makes them by the dozens for us and for friends around the country. He keeps them catalogued and even takes orders and requests. Each tape comes with his typed "music notes," listings and personal comments.

He's made several Big Band tapes, selections — his, of course — from Tommy Dorsey, Glenn Miller and Duke Ellington. After Ella Fitzgerald died, Bud sent me his tribute tape to her, beginning where she began with "A Tisket a Tasket."

He enjoys great arias, too, and now so can I, as the tapes accompany me on errands back and forth between work and home, between Oklahoma and Texas, between my life with Bud and my life since.

My favorites are his. He's up to "Bud's Favorites No. 12," 15 tunes including Nat King Cole's "Paradise," Sinatra's "The Second Time Around," "Tangerine" from Helen O'Connell (who?) and "Lazy River" by Hoagie Carmichael.

When Ol' Blue Eyes died, Bud made two tribute tapes: one of Frank's Broadway songs, one of his ballads. Bud can't get too much of Frank. His intro on one Sinatra tape goes like this: "This tape is for our friends Helen and Bob Schmidt. Helen says 'I'll Never Smile Again' is her favorite, so I found this version by Frank Sinatra and the Pied Pipers with the Tommy Dorsey Orchestra from 1945. So get ready for ol' Frankie Boy, Helen. Hope you enjoy it!"

Bud is a long, tall Texan with Panhandle sensibilities, a terrific handicap, a still-working work ethic, bred-in-the-bone optimism, a gentle love his family never doubts, and a way of coping with anything life hands him with an always-ready sense of humor. Except for the golf swing, I have learned everything I need to know from him.

He learned these values in a less complicated world, America in the Thirties, Forties and Fifties. Then music and entertainment were sweet, funny and carefree, and life felt more like soft shoe than heavy metal. Benny Goodman and Margaret Whiting lulled soldiers to sleep at night; Jack Benny and Bob Hope kept them laughing all day. Gangsta Rap didn't help then or now, because in spite of great calamity, Americans had the sun in the morning and the moon at night.

Father's Day came around this year, and after talking to Bud, I realized the gifts come from him. Better than the man who reaches into his pocket and hands his kids candy, or the flashy, raucous Dallasite who doles out stiff, new stock certificates, my Dad reaches into his conservatory, pulls out a tape and says, "I made this for you."

Bud's musical sidebars arrive as gifts for me. If I'm blue, maybe overwhelmed with my own job as a parent, I have only to slip one of his Favorites into my tape player and listen to Judy Garland (or could it be Bud?) telling me to forget my troubles, come on get happy.

A LITTLE MORE POP

FEBRUARY 1998

n 1902, a 12-year-old French-German boy and his 13-year-old sister left their home in Alsace-Lorraine and traveled by ship from America with nothing but the clothes they were wearing and the name of a man who might give them a job.

Eventually, the boy, Felix Mandell, settled in Texas, not far from another sister and brother who had immigrated some years earlier. His sister, Camille, found her way to New Mexico. But they never saw their parents again.

What Felix did see was 98 years of life that stretched from 1890 to 1988, from a tiny village in Europe to a hot, sprawling cow town in the American West, from that lonely trip across the sea to a family and friends who would surround and adore him the rest of his long life.

He died last week, my grandfather Pop, just hours after winning a big pot — about $2.50 — in his weekly poker game. He had not been sick or in pain. He had his disappointments, to be sure, and like most immigrants, he knew dislocation and struggle, loneliness and the feelings of an outsider. But as with many Europeans who settled in the West, America and Americans were good to him. By leaving Europe, he and his family escaped the destruction of European Jewry, bringing their hope and faith to a new world.

He had, very simply, just lived, and for him it was enough. *"C'est suffit,"* he said to me often and about many things. "It's enough."

I think that attitude may have been the reason he lived so long and so well. He never went to school after the fourth grade in France; he never learned to drive a car; he never owned a home or jewelry or furs or traveled much. Yet whatever he did or had was enough for him. He had his health, his love of baseball, a good job, a decent living, a family and many friends. He lived all of his adult life in the dusty, flat, but

73

friendly town of Amarillo, Texas.

And he did see two brothers named Wright try to lift a plane out of a field in Chicago one afternoon in the early 1900s. He saw the Chicago White Sox play in their heyday. He raised a son who graduated from college and became his lifelong companion. He was there for the births of his grandchildren and even great-grandchildren.

For 40 years he sold mens hats in Amarillo to friends and customers who came to the store as much for his charm and good nature as his handling of haberdashery.

"A man's not dressed without a hat," he'd say, never accepting the trend for men to appear bare-headed in public.

His days were simple, his needs uncomplicated, his humor warm and easy. His attitudes were tolerant, forgiving, hopeful and loving. His eyes smiled, his moustache twitched, his arms opened and everyone loved Pop.

Living modestly, he traveled through the Dust Bowl, the Depression and two world wars with no more baggage than he brought off that ship.

I don't think I can live like my Pop, coasting along, moving gently through time. But some days, when I barely have time to come up for air and everything I've always wanted isn't nearly enough, I hope that sheer genetics will prevail. I could do well with a little more of Pop.

PEANUTS AND CRACKERJACKS
OCTOBER 1978

t only took me a few pitches to fall in love with Mark Gardner. The starter for the San Francisco Giants kept the Chicago Cubs scoreless until the fifth inning of the one-game playoff for the National League wild card playoff slot, and though the Cubs were my team, I liked Gardner's dark, wavy hair and chiseled features.

The camera came in close. On the mound, he looked worried, but still tough and, I thought, great. Strong, bright eyes. Young but not silly. Loved the way his cap came down over his forehead.

He turned his head, and I got a better look at the aqualine profile.

Then he spit. But he didn't just spit. He actually wound up for the spit, turning his head way back over one shoulder, bringing it back to center and, with speed at least half that of his fastball, he let it sail, this hideous glob of whatever it was.

Oh, brother. That drove out Gardner – both for San Francisco and for me. Call me fickle, but call me finished with that spitter.

By now my attention was more on the game and less on the guy, anyway. Cubs' hitter Gary Gaetti broke the scoreless game wide open with a two-run homer followed by a triumphant bow from the dugout. Wow! Those loveable losers may get there yet!

What a hit! What a hitter! What a guy!

With fans cheering, "Guy-ett-tee! Guy-ett-tee!" he modestly returned to the dugout, sat down next to one of his teammates and exchanged a nod and two shakes. And then the two of them started to chew.

And chew they did. I found myself rubbing my own aching jaw watching in astonishment as they chewed and chewed, faster and faster, heads still but jaws a-pumpin'.

Gaetti has just broken this game wide open bringing his team back to life and these two just sit there like zombies and chew? Yech.

Cubs pitcher Steve Trachsel takes his time between pitches so the camera roams a lot. At this point, we got a nice shot of the Giants' dugout and Armando Rios — not a bad-looking fellow himself. Rios was leaning back against the wall, arms crossed in front, and I was fully enjoying the view. Then he stretched out, put his hands behind his head and after easily five full seconds of major league chewing, he blew the biggest, pinkest bubble I've ever seen.

At least you could see what he was chewing.

Another break, and we got a close-up of Orel Hirshiser, that sweet boy from Buffalo. I remembered when he was an all-American hero. An ace pitcher, Cy Young Award winner and a great all-around athlete. What a charming young man, I mused. I guessed Orel must not be playing much because he had on his shiny black Giants jacket, was sitting off to one side of the dugout kind of by himself and was, you got it, chewing.

But Orel was being much more than oral. He would reach down (below the screen) and — without even looking down! — toss something into his mouth. Once in his mouth, whatever it was got chewed up a little, spit out and in would go more. What the hell is that? I asked myself, squinting and edging closer to the TV. Peanuts? Was he shelling them with his teeth? Popcorn? Was he spitting out the kernels? Sure I was impressed with his eye-hand coordination, but more than a little grossed out.

By now the game was getting hot. The Giants were trailing 4-0 with two outs and the bases loaded. Manager Dusty Baker must have been tense, but the only sign was the toothpick he alternately chewed and flipped in and out of his mouth or balanced between his uppers and lowers. While I worried about the toothpick, he worried about the game.

Barry Bonds was up next. He's big, he's calm and he's got a cool earring. A choker in postseason, he'd been a great hitter and the Giants' best hope to get back in the game. I moved up to the edge of my seat.

Before Bonds gets into position, we see a lot of him. Against the background of the darkening Chicago sky. Warming up with two bats. The camera loves him at every angle and especially in close on this boyishly handsome powerhouse.

And at that pivotal moment when we see every pore and bead of sweat on his face, guess what? He spits, too. At least Gardner turned to one side. Highlighted by the combined luminosity of the television and the ballpark lights, Bonds just lets loose with full frontal spew. His slimy blast is long and hard and accompanied by an exploding spray.

After this show, his at-bat was anti-climactic for me. The three-time MVP grounded out to first, then, in another display of class and good taste, he slammed his helmet to the ground.

THE GUTS TO VOTE

September 1998

like unusual gifts. Not unusual like baby cheetahs or a trek in the Himalayas or a new Smith and Wesson but still, unusual. For example, when my son became 18, I hauled him down to a tag agency and asked him to register to vote. It took 20 minutes, total. I told him that, along with some CDs, this was his gift: his right to vote. We live freely, every day, I reminded both of us, because we can vote for or against the people who make our laws.

The value of this gift may not be obvious. But it may be the most valuable gift you ever get, I said. Your freedom — all of ours — depends on it. Please use it.

So, naturally, when my birthday came long, I hauled same son out of bed and this time drove him to a polling place.

The primary election this year in Oklahoma happened to be the day before my birthday. I want you to vote, I told him. Knowing that you voted, that you have actually done your duty, is the gift I want from you.

"Who do I vote for?" he asked. "Isn't it just a primary?"

I handed him the Oklahoma Gazette's special section on judicial races and The Sunday Oklahoman's voter guide.

"Read this," I said. "It's not everything, but it's something. And a primary sets up the fall election. Maybe we can get rid of some useless incumbents."

"Don't I need I.D?"

"Nope. It's easy. You're already registered. You just walk in, give your name, vote. They make it easy to vote in Oklahoma. So there's no reason not to."

We drove five blocks, parked and walked only about 30 yards to the entrance to Horace Mann School, the polling place for our precinct, gave our names, got our ballots, filled them out, put them in the counting machine, slapped "I Voted!" stickers to our lapels and that was it.

In only about 10 minutes — maybe 20, if you count the time it took to "become informed" — we had exercised that most basic of all democratic rights and most important responsibility. We had done something for our own freedom no less significant than what the president is doing by meeting with Boris Yeltsin or what Janet Reno is doing by examining alleged violations of campaign finance laws or what embassy employees are doing by risking their lives to serve the goals of democracy in East Africa.

We had given our consent to be governed, no small power that. But my son and I were among the measly 21 percent of registered voters in the state who accepted that responsibility, enjoyed that power and cast our votes on Aug. 25. That was the lowest voter turnout in a gubernatorial primary in Oklahoma in 50 years, matching a trend nationwide.

Oh, those politicians don't care what we think, you say, giving a reason for not voting. They only listen to money, big money, the media, each other, whatever. Why bother? They're corrupt, out of touch, amoral, immoral, dishonest, disconnected, irrelevant, out of line and you're out of patience with all of it

The economy's fine, you can't connect to politics, anyway, so you don't vote. Besides, there's nobody good to vote for.

Baloney. Lots of smart, hard-working, caring men and women are still running for office. Not everyone is disillusioned with public service or American politics. By not voting, you let them down. They have the guts to run; at least you can have the guts to vote.

These are not good reasons, they're excuses. If you just stay home and watch the people you complain about run, win, hold office and get re-elected, that is exactly what will happen. Some would even say you get who you deserve.

Don't you imagine that if, instead of 21 percent, 95 percent actually voted, you'd see politicians listening to those voters and not just their consultants?

That's the way it's supposed to work, the way it was meant to work and the only way it can work. Someone will govern, whether you like them or not, whether you get up off your can and do something about it or not.

Want to see what government and politics is like in America without the freedom and responsibility to vote? You are.

EPILOGUE

My son, Joey Fleischaker, now 24, did more than just vote in Oklahoma's 1998 primary election. In the 2000 presidential election campaign, he made himself useful to the managers of the Democratic National Convention in Los Angeles. That job then evolved into a four-month assignment in the Gore-Lieberman campaign traveling ahead of vice presidential candidate U.S. Sen. Joe Lieberman, D-Conn., on the advance staff, setting up meetings, rallies, press events and motorcades in cities across the country. He learned — from the inside out — what real politics in America is about.

He criss crossed the country, worked hard, slept little, ate junk on the run, was abused by power-hungry politicians and their power-hungry staff, or abandoned by inept campaign workers unused to the pressure, and I think he loved every minute of it. He's young, hungry himself and ready to rock 'n' roll. Not many of his contemporaries voted in this election, but I am proud to say that he did.

FIVE

BELLES, BOWS AND PANTYHOSE

THE BELLE OF BOWS
DECEMBER 1994

Whatever you did this weekend," said Katie Couric before introducing The Queen of Quaint, "it can't compare."

I could feel it. Martha Stewart was nearby. And Katie was talking to me. I am dead certain of that, because she was staring right at me while I brushed my teeth, held a cold pack over my dark, swollen eyes and slapped my cheeks around in my morning ritual-to-avoid-a-facelift.

It was the morning after our annual Chanukah party, which I thought had been wonderful. Co-hosted with another family, we invited friends, neighbors, Jewish families and those-who-get-to-have-a-Christmas-tree, too. We had lots of kids, Menorahs (candelabras) filled with glowing candles everywhere, traditional latkes (potato pancakes), Chanukah cookies and much good food contributed by our guests.

The kids took turns reading parts of the Chanukah story — a tale about freedom over tyranny — opened gifts, played a game of chance called Dreidl for candy coins and tortured each other gleefully. In all, it was a family values first-prize winner, and I'm still feeling warm and fuzzy when She comes into the picture.

I am knocked out by Martha Stewart. This so-called guru of glue-guns has taken entertaining, decorating, crafts, cooking and gardening to new levels of hysteria weekly on television, in books, magazines and certainly, at the bank. As she remakes chandeliers and glues acorn caps back on the darling little acorns ("The California variety are much nicer than those old things you find on the ground in New England!"), she skips right over the sublime and goes straight for ridiculous.

She was Katie's guest on the "Today" show that morning, showing

83

all of us how to "do the holidays." Even more chipper than usual, she'd been twirling around the White House, inspecting the Christmas finery and showing their Chief of Bowology a thing or two.

I stared at the screen, toothpaste drooling down my chin, terror in my eyes, as Martha and her sidekick demonstrated the hand-making of wreaths and balls for Christmas. The camera narrowed in on her helper's handiwork. He was sticking little red floral something-or-others into this "divine" ball covered with paper tape — better, don't you know, than plain ol' Styrofoam balls. Martha swooned at his side.

"I really love the jewel tones of these flowers," she entoned.

" We're making cockscomb balls."

I gagged on my toothpaste. But there was more.

"On to our elegant garlands." She said, "they're so wonderful."

"All you need are some pine cones; we're using the immature ones (meaning green) which you simply pop in the oven for 6-8 hours at 325 'til they're oh so nice and crisp.

"Then you turn to your drum-motor drill press," (mine is always at my side in the kitchen, isn't yours?) "and, using a $\frac{1}{16}$-inch drill bit, make a nice neat little hole in the end of the cone."

Moaning, holding my forehead in a sweaty palm, I am perched on the bathroom throne watching this nightmare and fighting off waves of insecurity.

Had our gathering been all it could have been? Should I have cooked pine cones instead of the turkey? Were the Safeway paper plates, ripped from their wrapper at chow time, not quite the right touch? Martha molds her butter into beautiful little flowers, bells or whatnot. I shuddered, remembering: here, in my own home, I had actually tossed a big tub of Fleischmann's extra-light margarine onto the table and stuck a plastic knife in it.

Maybe I should have painted oak leaves with gold paint and pressed them onto my napkins. Martha does. Maybe I should have built centerpieces of Spanish moss and sterling silver cranberries, filled them with cooked pine cones previously dipped in glittering gold, placed tiny clay candle holders made of antique shards from Tutankhamen's tomb around the edges and arranged itsy bitsy candles – made by pouring wax into leftovers from Rodin's original bronze moldings – into each and every one. Martha would have.

I stopped the self doubt long enough to see her turn to her handy helper. He had just finished weaving an 80-pound wreath of branches from trees flown in only yesterday from the Amazon rain forest and was now back at his post sticking stuff in Styrofoam.

"What else," Martha cheerfully asks him, "are you using for balls?"

DO-IT-ALL BARBIE

DECEMBER 1988

She's a ballerina, an island-fun girl, a perfume model, a surfer, a peaches 'n' cream girl. She even glows in the dark.

She comes equipped with a Corvette, California surfin' gear or an ice cream shop where she holds court. Her skirted vanity table is fully stocked with jewelry, makeup and a photo of Her Guy on whom she has been transfixed for at least 30 years.

Who is she, this wonder, this glamorous model of young womanhood? Is it Princess Di? Is it Madonna? It isn't Barbara Bush or Gwenyth Paltrow or even Flo Griffith-Joyner.

And it sure as hell isn't me.

It's Mattel's Barbie, almost the identical Barbie that I longed for in 1959 when I was given my first long-legged, well-shaped Barbie doll. This one wears more makeup and her wardrobe fits this era, not the Fifties, but she's the same gorgeous gal.

That impossible-to-attain figure. Those long, shiny golden locks — well, my Barbie was a brunette but, then, so was I.

Now my 5-year-old daughter longs for one. No, not just one. Today, the thing is to have lots of Barbies, and every little girl I know has or wants lots, too.

"Do I buy her one?" I ask myself pushing a shopping cart through the toy store. Barbie stands, or rather poses, for all those things many young girls and women want: beauty, charm, pretty clothes, perfect hair and makeup, a handsome boyfriend, the always-smiling face. Not bad. I'd take any one of those things myself.

But all girls don't come packaged that way — pretty, pert, perfect — and no amount of pretending will change that. Besides, this image of woman is nothing like the life my daughter is likely to choose for herself. While Barbie's clothes may fit today's fashions, her lifestyle doesn't. Don't they make lawyer Barbies, or Barbies wearing hard hats? Or teaching school? Or programming computers?

What about Barbies driving carpool frantically digging in their pocket books just to find their makeup? Do they make a lesbian Barbie?

If I encourage this fantasy life of Barbie's, will my daughter's real life be a disappointment? If the dream is beauty and boys, what will happen to brains and guts and being happy with herself just the way she is?

On the other hand (now I am pushing past the educational toy section), reality will hit plenty soon and for plenty long. Dreaming and pretending are some of life's best and most important private moments. Her fantasies really are none of my business. Whatever role she assumes, it should and will be hers to discover, hers to decorate and dress in whatever style fits her life and her time.

And like my friend said about buying his daughter's Barbie, "If they thought truck-drivin' Barbies would sell, believe me, they'd make them."

But wait! What do I see around the corner on the aisle marked "Girls Toys"? A doctor Barbie! She's wearing glasses, a white coat and has a stethoscope around her neck! So what if she changes into a glamour queen by night? Wrap her up; I'll take her.

Do-it-all Barbie may be fantasy, too, but this is a package I like.

GORGING ON GRAS

JANUARY 1996

aybe it was our cruising altitude of 30,000 feet. Maybe it was the sheer headiness of the luxury of traveling business class, but I had a dream somewhere over the Atlantic between the Strait of Denmark and the Labrador Sea from which I awakened terrified at the sound of my coronary arteries slamming shut.

I dreamed I was swimming – slogging, really – across the Seine, that muddied band of a river flowing oh, so romantically, so bitter-sweetly, so very Frenchly through Paris.

But wait. My Seine was not running with clear water, sparkling water, Evian or even Parisian sewage. The river of my dreams was nearly oozing with *foie gras.*

In my fancy, I was not only stuffed with this rich and distinctly European delight (*la femme farcie de foie gras*), I was totally surrounded by it (*foie gras en croute*), slicing through it (*foie gras farci*), and finally, drowning in it (*la mort par foie gras*).

No Freudian analyst need interpret this dream. I was returning from a week in France with my family, where we individually and collectively put away more thick slices of *foie gras* than there are guillotined revolutionary heads stockpiled at the Bastille.

When the first waiter at the first meticulously selected restaurant brought our first plates of this gastronomic treat, four sets of American eyes squinted with doubt. Clearly, this was not the chopped liver of Bar Mitzvah fame (made with bourgeois chicken livers); not really paté (much chunkier) and certainly not Oscar Meyer's Liverwurst Sausage (yuck). This, then, was something else; something to live and, quite possibly, die for.

Foie gras translates from French to English as "fat liver" and translates visually from a slice of meatloaf to a slice of smooth, creamy artistically blended paste of fattened goose or duck liver, cut to about one-half inch thickness and "crusted" with a great, golden glob of greasy, gelatinous goosey fat.

Foie gras is absolutely delicious in its unique, velvety way. It has the texture of smooth, ultra-rich butter laced with a mild gamy taste and enhanced, sometimes, by patterning the liver in stripes, squares or harlequins.

Foie gras apparently originated with the Egyptians in 2500 B.C. and is made by forcing geese and ducks to eat more than they normally would, a process perfected by nearly every American in Paris. Who knows what's happening to our livers, but the livers of these birds just get larger and larger and more and more succulent.

"The result," says David Rosengarten in the "Dean and DeLuca Cookbook," "is a creamy, fatty, ultra-seductive chew that sends a shiver down the spine of most diners."

I'll say. I've seen the spines of my diners — one teen-ager and one post — shiver over nachos, pizza or a Quarter Pounder with cheese, and their noses turn skyward at the mention of liver 'n' onions. But even these gringos were gorging on the *gras*.

In Paris, we were stuffed with *foie gras* before our entrees every single night for six successive nights. And on the seventh night, we rested. Actually, we kept on eating like the gluttonous little American piggies we had become — *crepes, coquilles, terrines, éclairs, brioche*, etc. — but on more *foie gras*, we declared a moratorium which lasted for all of one day, until we arrived in Alsace-Lorraine, home to the foiest of all gras. There we hoarded tins of it to cart home.

When those are gone, we'll be left to our own devices. I'm told they serve *foie gras* here in the city — made with imported goose liver — at La Baguette and sometimes at The Coach House. I wish I didn't know that.

Should we want to try rustling up some at home, we won't find organ donors. The practice of pumping up goose livers is prohibited in the United States. But one can buy whole fattened duck livers from the distributor, D'Artagnan (honest) at 1-800-DAR-TAGN or at Dean & DeLuca's store in New York.

I can't say enough wonderful things about this blend. It has the capacity to stop all conversation, to bring out the pride of French chefs. One refused to bring us bread before serving his own *foie gras* course produced from his own gaggle, lest we fill up on the bread first. It has the effect of inducing a kind of eyelid-drooping, sensual torpor on its gourmands, as the luscious liver melts in your mouth with the result, no doubt, of taking five years off your life.

So who cares? *C'est la vie avec foie gras.* Let's all revise our living wills. Leave Dr. Kevorkian at home. Life and death, please, by gorging on *gras.*

CONFESSIONS OF A CHOCOHOLIC
FEBRUARY 1991

Like any addiction, it consumes. Between fixes, I feel sad and lethargic.

I can't keep it at home because I can't be trusted. So late at night I roam the streets of my neighborhood trying to score off my friends. I heard there was a huge supply unloaded in Norman, Okla., last weekend, but I had to be locked up to stay away.

Why should I shake this habit? Of all my personal "isms" — cynicism, neuroticism, astigmatism, Judaism, feminism, liberalism — my favorite is chocoholism.

I am wild about, obsessed with, driven madly toward and made totally nuts by my intense and predictable cravings for chocolate. I don't just like or want chocolate. I really, really love it. And I really, really need it. I think about it a lot. I arrange private time to slip out and buy one — one can't hurt, can it? — chocolate turtle.

I am quick to accept party invitations from hostesses who are known for their chocolate bundt cakes or brownies. I steal Halloween bags from children, sorting out all the mini-Snickers, Milky Ways, Kisses and M&Ms. I go on Easter egg hunts if there's any hope of unearthing chocolate eggs, and I make sure to exchange holiday gifts with highly acclaimed fudge makers. Fudge, oh God. The best.

Now why is an already chubby girl like me double-fisting this stuff? One explanation is genetic coding. For centuries, my grandfather's family supplied its French village with rich, gooey *mousse au chocolate, gateau chocolate* and *chocolate parfait*. So who am I to deny this luscious lineage?

But time and over-breeding have diluted the familial continental palate, and I don't require Godiva, Neuhaus or even Toblerone. Oh, I like them, all right. *Mon dieu!*

But mine is the American way, and I am just as happy with a Hershey Bar, Nestles Crunch, Hostess chocolate cream-filled cupcakes, Double Stuff Oreos — hell, I'm happy with regular-sized Oreos — or Chips Ahoy. Strike the Ahoy. I eat the chips. I do get desperate.

"Hello?" I am panting through the phone late at night to my understanding friend and neighbor. "Do you have anything chocolate?"

She searches. "Only chocolate syrup," she says. "You know, for the kids' milk."

I steal out into the night carrying my spoon. The kids can drink plain milk.

Our city, oft-criticized for its limitations, does have rich, hidden treasures of chocolate ecstasy dotting the landscape like dark jewels, and believe me, I know where to find most of them.

Try Fudge Love at the 42nd Street Candy Store; chocolate donuts at the Donut Shop N.W. 63rd and Western; Chocolate Chewies at Ingrid's; brownies at ND Foods or the Urban Market; the chocolate bomb at Flip's; Devil's food birthday cake with fudge icing from Kamp's; chocolate-filled chocolate *éclairs* at La Baguette; or my grandma's Texas pecan Mexican chocolate sheet cake with fudge frosting at my house.

By the way, don't even mention white chocolate to me. Cooked up by some honky Pharisee, it is a pale pretender of the real thing.

If I've missed anything, by all means, let this chocoholic know.

PANTYHOSE BUYER SHOPS 'TIL SHE DROPS
JULY 1991

O ne size never has fit all. One size, in fact, has never fit me at all, but just when I thought I'd give it another try, an industry left unregulated for too long has shaken the very legs on which I stand.

I speak, miserably, of pantyhose. Enter the hosiery section of any department store and see if you, too, aren't brought absolutely to your knees by the impossible task of buying some.

My favorite shopping sidekick and I ran into our local department store just to pick up some off-white ones, with maybe a little pattern. I should have smelled trouble when my buddy asked me about my membership in The Club. I have known this woman for years. We are both Democrats, the Junior League wouldn't have us and Ellie Smeal burned our NOW cards years ago. I didn't know what club she meant.

"The Hosiery Club," she said. "It's great. Buy 12, get another pair free."

This club is certainly no support group; it is a scheme to make crazy every pantyhose buyer in America. Buy 12 pair of pantyhose? Twelve double-legged harnesses chosen from case after case of daunting options? Who would want 12 pair?

Style offerings alone include silky, silky-sheer, opaque, support, light support, reinforced toe, reinforced heel, sandalfoot, control top, light control top, bikini top, cotton crotch or any combination of the above. All this just to cover a few spider veins and cinch in a little cellulite.

And we're just getting to color, of which there are hundreds, described for example as "ecru," "snowflake" or "crystal" but never just "off white."

On to size, which includes "A," fitting everyone from pre-Kindergarten to newlywed; "B," which claims to work for ladies weighing anywhere from 110 to 150 pounds, no matter how short or how shaped; and "C" or "D," for gals who would be better off buying a giant Ace bandage and wrapping it around their thighs, because that's how queen-sized pantyhose worn by anyone other than queens feel anyway.

Now, remember. I just want off white with a little something in the way of pattern. Too soon I learn I can have dots, pinstripes, big stripes, chevrons, squares, squiggles, lines up the back, bows on the heel, rhinestones on the ankle. Flo Nightingale white is available, but apparently the one thing I cannot have is just a *little* pattern.

Taking in row after row of hosiery counters, my knees start to knock, I grab my package (one pair, one big gamble) which costs half my paycheck, and I flee, glad my bare legs are still working.

Another friend says she finds the shopping part not as bad as the wearing-them part.

"There are so many humiliations," she says, "like roll-at-the-top syndrome, contracted when you buy 'B' but should have bought 'C,' and the pantyhose slip down and last night's dinner is pushed up. I even went back to wearing a garter belt," she confessed.

"But that experiment failed the day my garters came unsnapped, loudly and painfully, in a management meeting."

Occasionally, hosiery sales ladies are willing to help you with the fine art of getting them on and off.

"Sit down, dear," says a woman you suspect cuts them off at the knees and rolls 'em down.

"Start with one foot (duh) and pull, pull, pull! until you have reached the knee, then begin with the other foot."

I'm already feeling pain at the pull, pull, pull part when she finishes off with, "Now we're halfway there so wiggle left! and pull! Right! Pull! Now, pull evenly and, voila! You're in!"

In and totally exhausted, I should add, and you haven't even started on the strapless bra.

There is one last pantyhose problem yet to be solved by industry — one shared equally, for once, by women and men. Getting into them in a hurry is bad enough, but getting out?

Edward Scissorhands, where are you when we need you?

SIX

CONFESSIONS FROM A
WHITE HOUSE SLEEP-OVER

CONFESSIONS FROM A WHITE HOUSE SLEEP-OVER

MARCH 1997

y cover was blown by The Daily Oklahoman and The New York Times, who printed the list of overnight guests at the White House. So I saw my choices as two: take the cyanide capsule I keep for such nightmares, or confess. Since I want to live long enough to repeat my sin many, many times, I will save the pill for another heinous act and confess:

I Spent a Night in the Lincoln Bedroom. By the way, I own the White House and all the bedrooms in it, as do you. We even own Lincoln's bed and all his old sheets, which I hope are changed frequently, given how many people have been camping out there lately. But enough about the décor.

I Spent a Night at the White House for several reasons.

Public Reason: I was invited. I had plans to be in Washington, D.C., and wanted to spend some time with old friends, POTUS and FLOTUS[1] who are busy, busy, busy and had no other time to see me.

Hidden Reason: POTUS was attempting to lure me into using my vast influence to secure a $17 grillion contribution from our local conservative publishing family, the Gaylords, to either the Clinton-Gore re-election campaign or the Democratic National Committee.

Public Reason for Accepting: My schedule was also crowded. I was in D.C. to see old friends and to eat as many steamed Maryland blue crabs as I could find in one week. Being an old FOHAB[2], I also thought it would be fun to sit up and gab half the night with my friends.

Hidden Reason for Accepting: Secretly, clandestinely, passionately

[1] President of the United States and First Lady of the United States
[2] Friend of Hillary's and Bill's

and most definitely in a calculated manner, I was hoping that Mandy Patinkin, Paul Newman or some other Hollywood don would mistakenly but luckily have been booked into the Lincoln Bedroom that same night. You see, there's only one bed. I know this because I went. Yes, indeedy, I did.

In fact, I spent 24 hours there, most of it alone and trying to sleep. For the record, the following should account for all of my time there:

8 p.m. — 11:30 p.m. I alternately and frequently read the Gettysburg Address and browsed through the guide booklet that explains the antiques in the Lincoln Bedroom (In America, they're antiques. In Europe, they would be passed over at a flea market as too new.) I thought about playing Chopsticks or the Rach 2 on the piano in the hallway, but was too nervous. I thought about snooping around other parts of the White House, but was too nervous. I thought about asking for food, but was too nervous and wanted to call lots of friends long distance to tell them where I was, but was too nervous.

So I read my crappy detective novel to calm myself and wondered where the hell my old friends were.

11:30 p.m. — 12:30 a.m. — FLOTUS arrived. We had a nice talk about husbands, kids and jobs, and she went to bed.

12:30 — 1:30 a.m. — POTUS arrived, found me snoring on a settee in the hallway and peeled the crappy detective novel off my nose. We put our feet up and sat around talking about kids, parents, jobs, our health, our friends and our enemies. He likes to talk more than she does, even more than I do. It was nice to have some time together.

1:30 a.m.—7:30 a.m. Slept badly, clinging stiffly to four inches of Lincoln's bed and battling civil war ghosts. Awoke and ate my low-fat bagel with jam — ordered the night before and delivered with quiet style and unobtrusive elegance — drank decaffeinated coffee alone, read three important newspapers, showered and dressed. POTUS stopped by to say good-bye, see ya, and I left for my hotel, where I tried to get some sleep.

Noon. Resumed the eating of steamed Maryland blue crabs with a mutual FOB and FOP.[3]

Neither Paul nor Mandy were at the White House, nor was any attempt made by anyone to tap into my well-known stash of $50,000-$100,000 campaign contributions.

We didn't talk about campaign finance reform, and I doubt POTUS, FLOTUS or the MOCs[4] will be either, at least in any meaningful way. Power and greed are not solely the private properties of corporate America.

We did finally, the Chief Executive and I, have time to talk about the things real friends talk about so, in that way, I personally am glad POTUS was "ready to start the overnights . . ."

When Clinton and I and my husband and all of our mutual friends were kids just starting out in politics in Washington, we came and went from each other's houses all the time. But now he's living in a place with more security, and contrary to GOP opinion, it's hard to get a sleep-over there: A fat check isn't enough.

I tried to call Mr. Gaylord at his newspaper office when I returned to Oklahoma City to tell him the White House coffee is damned good, should he want to buy a cup for $17 grillion. He hasn't returned my call.

[3] Friend of Pam's
[4] Members of Congress

EPILOGUE

In an attempt to convince the public that the president was cutting the corners of campaign finance laws, the Republican National Committee and its henchmen made a very big deal out of the Clintons' practice of inviting guests to spend the night at the White House and giving them the special privilege of staying in one of the formal guest rooms, the Lincoln Bedroom or the Queen's Bedroom.

Some of those guests were indeed major donors to the Democrats and to the President's re-election campaign, and that's how they got "found out."

I just proudly signed the guest book.

GOP HOLY WAR
FEBRUARY 1999

In the absence of principles or policies to call their own, the Republican Party has become obsessed with scolding us.

Beset with the mission of trying to bring down the president, consumed by the "rightness" of its narrow views (eg: on abortion: no abortions, no way, no how) and caught up in its perceived duty to Bring Christian Values into each and every one of our lives, this campaign is a strange and risky one. American's don't much like politicians anyway, especially if they think they're dictating a moral code.

Maybe they'll paint themselves in a corner too tight and too far right to escape.

Maybe they'll be forced to reveal more nasty truths about their own sexual misconduct or be outed from their phony heterosexual closets or denied the right to leer 'n' sneer at Monica in public, or, best of all, be rejected by the voters in the next election.

Maybe we'll soon come to our senses and see this crowd of clowns for what it really is — preachy, moralistic, self-righteous and, as conservative theorist David Frum puts it, headless. Or maybe like their counterparts, these zealots will become whirling dervishes, spinning themselves into oblivion. One can only hope.

Today's new right-wing Republicans (Will any others please stand up?) failing to follow through with their promises in the once-popular Contract with America, failing to win much in the 1998 congressional elections and failing to articulate their goals for themselves as a party or us as a nation, are left headless, helpless, heedless and sometimes it seems, heartless.

As a result, they have become the Party of Impeachment, focusing entirely on pinning the tail on the donkey in the White House to the growing impatience and disgust of the public.

In fairness, they do have some plans: save children by making abortion illegal — Does this include bombing them into it? Bend and twist those nasty, scary homosexuals, back, back! into the purity of heterosexuality — Does this include beating them into it? Pass a flat tax, pay people to leave the public schools, etc.

But while the GOP has been harangueng sinners and converting everyone to Christianity, the Democrats have made real progress on the rest of the Republican agenda, admittedly at the GOP's nudging, like reforming welfare, balancing the budget and reducing crime. So what's a party to do? Especially the Party of Uptight White Guys, as Georgia's GOP chair calls it.

Declare war, of course. In the absence of anything real and helpful, why not a jihad? A moral crusade that scorns non-believers, bullies moderates, patronizes women, cracks down on immigrants, makes sure everyone buys at least one gun and trots out humorless hangmen like Reps. Bob Barr, R-Ga., and Tom DeLay, R-Texas, to remind us that they — and they alone — know the difference between good and bad, evil and virtue, Lot and Mrs. Lot.

So where has traditional, authentic conservatism gone amidst all this moralizing? By waging a holy war of impeachment as "a case not so much for the President's public legal impropriety but for a private, moral iniquity . . . [conservative intellectuals] have created a conservatism become Puritanism, a conservatism that has long lost sight of the principles of privacy and restraint, modesty and constitutionalism, which used to be its hallmarks," wrote Andrew Sullivan, a contributor to The New York Times Magazine.

What we are left with is some mutation of the once-rich conservative mind, observes Sullivan. What we are left with are men and women, but mostly men, who spend their time and our money writing laws, deposing young, thong-wearing women and debating everyone else's moral rectitude in the guise of representing our interests.

Leave it alone, guys. You may be comfortable squeezing your consciences into that ever-shrinking box, but I'm not. And while I may be willing to give up my tax dollars, my privacy and my social security benefits, I am certainly not willing to give up my conscience.

EPILOGUE

In 1998, the U.S. House of Representatives debated the impeachment of a president for the first time since the Watergate scandal of 1974.

The House voted to approve two of the four articles of impeachment brought against President Bill Clinton in matters relating to his relationship with White House staffer Monica Lewinsky.

"Following a trial that began on January 7, 1999, and consumed 14 days of arguments by lawyers for the House and Clinton plus three days of closed-door debate among Senators, the Senate on February 12 rejected the two articles of impeachment from the House; the Constitution required a two-thirds vote to convict, and therefore the president was not removed from office."

The Almanac of American Politics, 2000
Michael Barone, Grant Ujifusa

FROM HO-HUM TO HISTORIC
AUGUST 2000

n August 1984, I stood just off the podium at the Democratic National Convention in San Francisco and watched history being made.

Geraldine Ferraro, a member of the U.S. House of Representatives from Queens, New York, was named by then-Democratic presidential candidate Walter Mondale to run with him for vice president of the United States.

It was a first: The first time a woman had been seriously considered for a national ticket, the first time a woman had accepted and run.

"Gerry! Gerry!" screamed thousands at that gathering and at every stop along the campaign trail for the next three months.

Women and men, but especially women, felt a special pride in this choice. Ferraro was smart, energetic and tough. She represented the best in us.

"It's a girl!" reported National Public Radio anchor Linda Wertheimer, with apparent glee. "Only in America!" we hollered back.

Ferraro and Mondale did not win the match, but women won the point.

Last Monday, another point was made, this time by the likely Democratic nominee for President, Vice President Al Gore, with another uniquely American choice. By selecting U.S. Sen. Joseph Lieberman, D-Conn., as his running mate, Gore has moved this otherwise depressing presidential race from the ho-hum to the historic.

To some, Lieberman is an "intellectual's intellectual."

Educated at Yale University — so was George W. Bush — and Yale law school, Lieberman adds his brains to Gore's, yet he brings a warm, self-deprecating humor to the somber Democratic picture. His character, integrity and values are unquestioned. His leadership abilities are strong. His political value, of course remains to be seen. But I think he's a plus for the ticket.

A deeply religious and observant Orthodox Jew, Lieberman is the Democrats' answer to the self-righteousness of the Religious Right. He's the bold move Gore needed to make on the heels of the splashy GOP convention.

He's a grown-up, something George W. still is not, and something Gore may be but doesn't look like. Lieberman moves the focus away from the Clinton administration and on to a new American dream — putting someone from a minority, in this case a Jewish person, in a position to become president.

And as one GOP strategist put it, "It puts Florida back in play." The Democrats might have written off that big state to the Bushes — Shrub's brother Jeb is Florida's governor — but now the huge Jewish population there could vote Democrat just to have one of its own in office.

Jews have held office in America in increasingly large numbers in the last decade.

There are 11 Jewish members of the U.S. Senate; both senators from California are Jewish and more than 100 Jews serve in the U.S. House. But the choice of Lieberman makes it easier to imagine the acceptance of strong Jewish candidates elected from less likely places — even Oklahoma, as Democrat state Treasurer Robert Butkin considers a race here for governor.

And it brings the possibility of electing members of other minority groups to national office closer to reality.

Certainly there will be anti-Semitic sentiments expressed against Gore and Lieberman, overtly or more subtly, as there were against a woman or would be against someone black, Hispanic or Asian.

But I have confidence in American voters. I think we like our diversified democracy. I think we're proud of the fact that a woman or a Jewish man could, like Catholic John F. Kennedy did, be elected to one of the highest offices in the land.

EPILOGUE

As it turned out, the choice of Joe Lieberman as a running mate was an inspired moment for Al Gore. Lieberman spent lots of time campaigning in Florida, playing to adoring crowds of older, Jewish voters. The vote there was so close — indeed, just a few hundred votes officially separated the Gore-Lieberman ticket from Bush and Cheney in Florida — there can be little doubt that Lieberman was a key factor.

And the senator did bring the note of humanity and good humor apparently lacking in the Democratic ticket. Of the four debates during the election season, the Lieberman vs. Cheney match was the only one where the candidates were statesmanlike, each addressing the issues and each other with respect, knowledge and high-mindedness.

THEY'LL GET OVER IT

DECEMBER 2000

"He hurts like a brother, seeing the trials of his own flesh and blood."

his quotation is not mine. Surprisingly, it isn't the Rev. Jesse Jackson's or Pat Robertson's or Pat Buchanan's, either. It isn't biblical, nor is it a line from either "The Exorcist" or "The Gladiator."

It is the Quote of the Day from the Friday, Dec. 8, New York Times, intoned by our very own Gov. Frank Keating, after he had spent what must have been a heart-wrenching night at the governor's mansion in Tallahassee, Fla., with Shrub's now-dishonored brother, Weed.

Good grief, Frank, get a grip.

Sure this is a hard time for the Bushes, the Gores, the Cheneys, the Liebermans and anyone else who assumed Election Day would be finished up around 2 or 3 a.m. All this uncertainty has gotta be hard on the Bush family – hard not to know if your next job will be running the state of Texas or the United States of America.

Hard not to know if you should be paying close attention in those daily intelligence briefing sessions or if, whew, they were just in case. Hard not to know who to put on the staff list, when to make the Cabinet calls, how to act presidential without, well, panting.

Hard not to know if the girls should get inaugural gowns appropriate for mild Austin winters or harsh Washington snowstorms. Hard not to know just how much, or maybe too much, brother Jeb did for you and the family.

But bloodletting between brothers? Trials to tear apart a family? Methinks our governor, and maybe the Bush Boy governors as well, hath lost perspective.

These people, these Bushes and Gores, are not, after all, homeless or jobless or battling Ebola. Hell, they probably all have tickets to the

Orange Bowl, which is more than most Okies have even though practically every single voter here cast his and her ballot – undimpled – for George W. Bush.

This is just a little family feud, Frank. The Big Bush is either burning or sad, depending upon who asks him; the Shrub is chomping at the bit, but scared as a jackrabbit; and the Weed doesn't know what hit him.

As for the Gores, they can't see the forest for all these bushes. But they can only blame themselves, having no brothers around to take the fall. By the end of January, they'll all get over it.

As for me, I think it's been great. I have been marching around my kitchen, talking to, yelling at and laughing with my television set for one month.

I love watching journalists try to keep up with real news, lawyers forced to get their facts straight and spinners, like Keating, spinning themselves into hilarious hissy fits.

In the meantime, we bystanders are watching sausage being made from a bit of democracy, some law, a lot of political maneuvering and a little constitutional flavoring.

This post-election circus has been fascinating, aggravating, encouraging and discouraging all at once, and you bet, it's been important. But please, Mr. Keating. He hurts like a brother? Life does go on, even for the Bushes and the Gores. No one's bleeding. No one "on trial" in the Florida recount faces the death penalty – or any kind of penalty at all, for that matter.

We'll see one guy become president and another guy, we hope, be a big boy about losing. We'll see four years of a White House full of folks who got there on a wing and a prayer, and eventually we may know who won – who really won.

But, wait! There's another new game in town. The Congress! The nasty, too-close-for-comfort, down-and-dirty, ever-partisan Congress. Won't that be something to see? Let the games begin!

GOVERNOR POP-OFF
OCTOBER 1996

Memo: To one big mouth
From: Another

Governor Keating: (a.k.a. Frank, Too Frank)

Excuse my boldness, but I can't help but noticing that you have, particularly of late, let loose with a few fatuous phrases that deserve reviewing. They probably ought to be tanked along with the pathetic sound bite/speechwriter who wrote them.

Some date back to your early months in office and were written off as the goofs of a still-green governor. But now it's getting to be a habit and certainly not a nice one.

Because these quips may give us a picture of your multiple personalities — excuse me, multiple roles — and are educational for we, your people, I have categorized them. Of course, they are taken out of context, but these doozies are bad even as stand-alones.

The Ethnically Sensitive Frank Keating

"Sometimes I humorously say that being a Catholic Republican in Oklahoma in 1995 is like being a black in Selma, Alabama, in 1943."
What a sense of humor! Is this your take on the civil rights movement?

The Imperial Frank Keating

"Aluminum windows may be fine for your house, but not for the governor's mansion." This was your explanation for spending $90,000 in state funds to tear out new aluminum window frames and replace them with wood ones. Try plywood. It works for your neighbors.

Also. "It's like my daughter who just graduated from college. She wanted a convertible with leather seats, but all we could afford was a convertible with cloth seats. Good Republican cloth seats."

I know, I know. You were trying to compare state government spending to a recent gift given to your daughter. But this is what happens when a Republican tries to explain government spending.

The Insulting Frank Keating

"She is the bag lady of the Democratic Party, . . . the chairman of the Flat Earth Society. She howls at the moon. She has no credibility and never will."

Whoa, Frank. Mild-mannered state Democratic Party chair Betty McElderry sure pushed your buttons. She only wondered how you could justify raising $700,000 to refurbish the mansion. Next time, stay cool and sic your decorator on her.

Then: "Because the other . . . teachers are slugs." This was your reply to a question explaining a hypothetical program offering bonuses to some teachers but not to others. Makes you wonder what it is about education you do like. The rotten apple award to you for this one.

The Diplomatic Frank Keating

"Obviously, we still have a bunch of dunderheads . . . in the Legislature."

So it's not the most popular bunch in the state. Your job is to work with them, remember? For the common good, remember? The last governor who forgot that had to tell it to the judge.

Then: "I didn't vote for the guy of course, but he has responded well to our crisis in Oklahoma City."

This appreciative remark was made in a live national TV interview just hours after the Murrah Building bombing and was about requesting federal aid from President Clinton, the aforementioned guy. Luckily, he didn't hold your oddly-timed dig against you or you against us.

And let's not forget this jibe: "The Micron people are 'yuppies.' They're mountain people. That's why they'll probably pick Utah over Oklahoma."

These helpful insights were given while Oklahoma was trying to recruit a multi-million dollar computer company that ultimately did, yesiree, pick Utah over Oklahoma for its new plant and 3,000 new jobs. But, hey, you've already got a job, so why worry?

About that job, Governor. Your most recent off-the-cuff comments on what makes our state great may be helpful to voters wondering whether to re-hire you. Trying to make a case for lowering taxes and encouraging growth, you expressed confusion that while we do well in sports and at beauty pageants, we are still the fourth poorest state in America. The next time you have to contend with this paradox, try this: Give aluminum window frames to the athletes, convertibles to the beauty queens and 3,000 new jobs to the teachers. They'll love you for it.

HER WORDS, HIS ANGER
OCTOBER 1991

PROLOGUE

In the fall of 1991, Clarence Thomas, a former chair of the U.S. Equal Employment Opportunities Commission and a conservative, Republican, African-American man, was nominated by President George Bush to fill an opening on the U.S. Supreme Court. During confirmation hearings before the U.S. Senate Judiciary Committee, University of Oklahoma tenured law professor Anita Hill, an African-American woman, emerged as a reluctant witness against Thomas.

Hill, an Oklahoman from Lone Tree, graduated from Oklahoma State University and Yale Law School before serving in Washington, D.C., as a staff member under Thomas in the Office of Civil Rights at the U.S. Department of Education and at the EEOC, as well. She joined the OU law faculty in 1986 and for five years taught several courses there, including commercial law, contracts and a course called Race & Racism in American Law.

At the Senate hearings, Hill described Thomas' repeated, inappropriate and disturbing behavior toward her during the time she worked for him. While not specifically labeling it sexual harassment, she strongly implied his behavior was clearly that. Thomas denied her charges and, in so many words, said she was lying.

The tone of the hearings became hostile all the way around. Accusations of exaggerations, grinding axes, lying and "playing the race card" were leveled at both the witness and the nominee. Women's and civil rights groups, anxious that Hill be heard and taken seriously, were offended at the committee members' belittling treatment of Hill and said so publicly and frequently. Thomas' defenders enjoined the battle to blast Hill and her supporters on the committee. Without an actual fisticuffs, it was, nevertheless, an ugly brawl.

Thomas was confirmed by the U.S. Senate on Oct., 15, 1991, by just four votes — 52-48. The Oxford Guide to the Supreme Court called it "the smallest margin of approval in more than one hundred years."

F rom the beginning, I was bothered by the depths of Clarence Thomas' anger. Since he was nominated to a position on the U.S. Supreme Court in August, I thought that someone so bitter and unresolved about his own conflicts could not be relied upon to resolve the conflicts of a nation.

I thought his resentment of white people had turned him away from black people, and that conflict, naturally, left him angry. I thought the undeniable anguish of his childhood had turned him away from people with similar backgrounds and left him angry at those who emerged less scarred than he.

I thought the unswerving rightness with which he presented his own judicial philosophy, the no-chinks-in-the-armor image, the barely controlled emotion, boiling out at just the right moments — added up to a man who was a long way from coming to terms with the inequities, disappointments and pain of being a black man in America.

How dare you, he seemed to say, accuse a man of my humble and painful beginnings of any wrongdoing? How dare you suggest, he asks with totally believable hurt, that someone treated so unfairly by life could treat anyone else unfairly? How dare you cause more suffering — you Anita Hill, you senators, you reporters — to one who has suffered so much?

After watching nearly every minute of the proceedings of his confirmation hearing before the U.S. Senate Judiciary Committee, I am convinced that Thomas' seething rage is more than justifiable anger at injustice, poverty and bigotry. To me, it is more a cover-up of flaws he cannot accept in a flawed world, let alone in himself. So he displaces all that rage and turns it on anyone who would threaten him. This anger has had a kind of blinding effect on his supporters, too, who carry his moral indignation for him, turning every question or suggestion of his possible weakness as a man into a travesty against his honor.

The defense of Thomas went something like this: Because this man has had such a hard life, and because no one ever saw him misbehave, he is not capable of this misbehavior, so this terrible invasion into his actions is not as much a search for the truth as it is more hardship for him.

He couldn't possibly be lying, they said with absolute certainty, because someone who has overcome such great odds doesn't deserve this final injustice. What right, they asked, does Anita Hill or any of you have to suggest this of such a man?

As if he were the only person in the limelight ever to have his private life made public. As if he were the first person to have reporters snooping around his house. As if he were the only person ever accused of sexual harassment.

The clearest evidence of his misdirected anger came when he played the racial card. The proceedings, he said, "are a high-tech lynching of uppity blacks." Where does he get that?

As one who is usually too quick to suspect racism in any difficult situation for minorities, even I thought the hearings were remarkably free of race-based bias. Racist motives had not once been suggested during any part of the proceedings. Not by Hill, not by the Senate committee, not by the groups opposing Thomas, not by the White House or even by the conservative groups supporting him. All the suggestions of racism, including the discussion of stereotypes about black men and sex, came from Thomas himself, giving pious proof that the world was, always had been, out to get him.

Now if Anita Hill had been white, we would have indeed heard cries of racism. And if, instead, Clarence Thomas had been white we probably wouldn't have heard Anita Hill at all.

Yes, I too, would be outraged if someone told lies about me before every man, woman and child in America. But I would also have to be outraged if someone told a terrible truth, or even some part of the truth, and humiliated me before that same audience.

It wasn't so much her word against his, as it was her word against his self-righteous anger.

EPILOGUE

Clarence Thomas received a full hearing on a range of issues, but the testimony from Anita Hill became so sensationalized, divisive and paralyzing for the Judiciary Committee and the Senate, the entire episode became known as "the Thomas-Hill hearings."

Back home, several members of the Oklahoma Legislature became angry at both Hill and the OU College of Law for allowing Hill to speak on its property — she initially spoke to the press about her upcoming testimony from a room at the law school. Led by State Rep. Leonard Sullivan, R-Oklahoma City, attempts were made in the state House to have Hill fired and the law school discredited, including the introduction of legislation to abolish the school. The dean and administrators of the school, including OU President David Boren, tromped up to the state Capitol to talk some sense into Sullivan, and the legislation died somewhere along the way.

At the same time, supporters of Hill — led by a group of women in Minnesota —raised a significant amount of money to endow a teaching position at the law school in her name. Motivated to honor Hill's role in speaking out against Thomas and to help secure her professional position, the group raised the prescribed amount of funds required by the state Legislature to match the private donations with state funds. By that time, however, the Legislature would hear nothing of it. The university did not fight to keep the funding for the position, and the idea died a painful, politicized death.

After Thomas' confirmation, Hill finished the ongoing law school term, then was granted a year-long sabbatical during which she gave a few interviews to the national media but mostly stayed away from public attention. She then returned to her teaching post at OU for several years and left in 1994. Today, Hill is teaching Race and Discrimination Law to PhD students as part of a series she designed entitled Law & Society at the Heller Graduate School at Brandeis University in Waltham, Mass.

HO HO HO. FA LA LA.
HERE'S YOUR GIFT. HA HA HA.

DECEMBER 1999

 book lover, are you? Then get ready. I've searched the bookstores, the web, the libraries and the newsstands, and some of these titles just beg to be my holiday gifts to you. A book it is said, is like a good friend. And for some on this list, maybe the only friend.

For that always-say-die guy, Dr. Jack Kevorkian, I picked up "Keep Your Brain Alive" by Lawrence Katz and Manning Rubin. It's a guide to keeping your mental muscles going while you're in confinement.

For Naomi Wolfe, one of Al Gore's top female advisers and the darling of the neo-classical/feminist/phooey movement, I couldn't resist buying "I'd Scream Except I Look So Fabulous" by Cathy Guisewite.

To Oklahoma's Gov. Frank Keating — who might have written it himself — "The Art of Doing Nothing" by Veronique Vienne.

To Vice President Al Gore, who, hard as he tries, can't overcome whoever it is that he is, Scott Adams' Dilbert collection of "Seven Years of Highly Defective People."

For George W. Bush, "The Oval Office for Dummies."

For Bye-Bye-Pat Buchanan, "Brain Droppings" by George Carlin.

The NASA space team, Mars division, seems already to have read Pritchett & Muirhead's "The Mars Pathfinder Approach to 'Faster-Better-Cheaper.'" I think it was a bad choice. Additional reading is in order, beginning with Pasachoff's "A Field Guide to the Stars and Planets," or failing that, "Mars Mystery: The Secret Connection Between Earth and the Red Planet" by Graham Hancock. Cheer up boys: That probe's bound to show up eventually. Just remember last year's best seller, "Women Are from Venus . . ." and men, oh you know, are from that other place.

Richard Carlson's "Don't Sweat the Small Stuff — and It's All Small Stuff" is my gift to Oklahoma City Mayor Kirk Humphreys as he contends with the challenges of the Central Hockey League, local businesstype Jim Brewer and the Oklahoma City Council.

"Brief Interviews with Hideous Men" by David Foster Wallace will be a wonderful gift, I think, for that pervert-turned-pundit Dick Morris.

To the police gang involved in the local Glitterdome scandal, a novel-cum-how-to-book called "Midnight in the Garden of Good and Evil" by John Berendt.

For Oklahoma County's district attorney, try-em-'til-they're-more-than-dead Bob Macy, please read "Letting Go." Then do it.

Howard Norman's "The Museum Guard" will make nice reading for New York Mayor Rudolph Giuliani.

"The Fury of the Northmen" by John Marsden goes, of course, to Minnesota Gov. Jesse Ventura. His day will come, but hopefully after mine has gone.

To the members of the Oklahoma Textbook Committee in celebration of their passing a disclaimer to be included in textbooks reminding us all that creationism is a valid theory, I offer several selections. Apparently, they've all read, "All I Really Need to Know I Learned in Kindergarten" by Robert Fulghum. But please don't stop there. I suggest the group take up the childrens' classic "Curious George" and its accompanying, adorable vine-swinging stuffed toy. After they've finished "George," they can begin, and hopefully end with, "A Confederacy of Dunces."

"Elves, Gnomes and Other Little People: A Coloring Book" by John O'Brien seems tailor-made for H. Ross Perot. He always stays in the lines.

Author Dr. Wayne W. Dyer couldn't have penned a better choice for local censor Bob Anderson and his vigilant vigilantes at Oklahomans for Children and Families than his treatise on "Your Erroneous Zones."

"The Goddess in the Office" is a must-read for any future employment situation for Monica Lewinsky, and I know she'll especially appreciate the gift from an old FOB.

Former state Rep. Charles Key, R-Oklahoma City, is our own devoté of Roswell. He should enjoy "UFOs Are Real" by Clifford E. Stone.

"Other People's Dirt: A Housecleaner's Curious Adventures" was written by Louise Rafkin but almost certainly belongs under the tree of America's First Faux Friend, Linda Tripp.

Two books, "How to Dump your Wife" and "Winning at Everything no Matter Who or How You Crush to Get There," are both anonymously contributed by former Wall Street magnates turned Las Vegas male hookers as personal guides for Donald Trump.

I'll bet the Clintons can hardly wait to crack open, "Bill and Hillary: The Marriage" by Christopher Anderson. It offers one more opinion on the couple's nearly 30 years together. How valuable these insights will be for them.

Every time I asked a guy his choice for on this title, it came up hands down Pamela Anderson. So she is the winner of "The Headless Bust" by Edward Gorey.

Jeff Foxworthy was just in town and left some copies of his book, "You Might Be a Redneck If . . ." I think it would be an appropriate addition to the reference collection at The Daily Oklahoman and just the right gift from me, along with this recommendation: Excerpts could replace your paper's daily, front-page prayer.

SEVEN

RIGHTS VS. MIGHT

CHOOSING LIFE
APRIL 1999

Seven a.m. on my daughter's 16th birthday, and I am sitting in a state patrol test center while she takes her driver's test for the much-anticipated license to freedom. Tonight, we plan to go to her favorite local restaurant and on the weekend, we'll have some of her friends over for hamburgers and gooey ice cream and cake in the back yard.

She's happy. She's loved. She's alive. She is lucky to be all of those things, and she is just beginning to know it.

Kids who have come into this test center to get their licenses are actually galloping. A license! Maybe a car! No more begging rides from Mom and Dad. A ticket to ride, and life is looking up.

I sit here, watching and smiling, knowing these happy, goofy kids can't possibly realize yet what a hassle car payments and repairs and traffic and tickets and maybe car accidents are going to be. They can't imagine a mother's anxiety as her daughter is turned loose behind the wheel of a machine capable of destruction, or a father's worry as she now spends hours away from home, on her own.

There is so much my daughter cannot know yet. So much joy and satisfaction waiting for her, but so much sadness and despair, too. Lots of decisions for her to make, lots of choices about the way she will make them and how she will live her life.

David Packman, the rabbi from my congregation, Temple B'nai Israel in Oklahoma City, talks about these choices in Freudian and in biblical terms, first explaining "libido" – our creative, productive, joyfully alive side – and "thanatos" (Greek for death), our destructive, dark and evil side.

"We have both," said Packman.

"As parents, our job is to try to strengthen libido and undercut the power of thanatos. We can't always stop it, that impulse to destroy, but we must be vigilant."

Yesterday, when my daughter was still 15, I watched the events at Columbine High School in Littleton, Colo., stunned, then angry, then heartsick. Still today, our heads spin with disbelief about these terrible murders, the boys who caused them, the kids who taunted those boys, the parents who raised those boys, the images that attracted and entertained them.

I am dragged down by despair, confused and frightened by this. If I can't understand, how can a 16-year-old bouncing around in Converse tennis shoes and cut-offs?

"These kids," said the rabbi, speaking of the perpetrators of the Colorado murders, "were attracted to the 'thanatos' of life, represented by Hitler, by the color black, by destructives games . . . their parents didn't necessarily cause it, but we cannot allow it.

"Suicide is the death of libido and the triumph of thanatos," he told me. "We have all known at least moments of that depression and despair. But we have to beat it back or simply get through it."

On days like yesterday when 14 kids and one adult were killed by someone else's "thanatos," when my own soft-eyed child is trying to grow up in a world gone nearly mad, it's not easy to beat it back. While she skips with carefree optimism around the corner of adolescence, I know what dangers lie on the other side.

Sometimes I ask myself: In the face of this horror, what does she want with this freedom? Why try to do well or be good? Why go to school? Why even go out the front door? Why teach them to struggle against hate when a classmate is teasing, taunting, torturing? Why teach them to resist fear when classmates have guns? Really; why bother?

In a world where this week's violence tops last, where children viciously end each other's lives and then their own, where signs of sadness and hatred were all around but parents seem not to have noticed,

I have to help her choose hope and choose life. For her, for now, it's as simple as a driver's license and a birthday party. But for me, I have to dig deeper.

The rabbi also reminded me of one of Judaism's strongest tenets, one that speaks to our source of deep-down, ages-old optimism. (For attribution, this is God speaking in Deuteronomy, read at Yom Kippur, the Day of Atonement.)

"... I have set before you today, life and prosperity, death and adversity ... choose life so that you and your descendants may live."

SAVING WOMEN'S LIVES
NOVEMBER 1995

ighteen months ago, Viki Wilson, a nurse, and her physician-husband Bill were expecting their third child," says an ad aimed recently at members of Congress considering a ban on late-term abortions.

"Early tests showed the pregnancy to be normal. But in the eighth month, ultrasound showed the fetus had a fatal condition." In fact, two-thirds of the baby's brain was lodged in a separate sack.

"Carrying the pregnancy to term could imperil Vicki's life and health," the ad went on, re-telling the Wilsons' story in a plea with Congress not to ban the medically necessary procedure.

"On the advice of their doctor, Viki and Bill made the heart-breaking decision to have an abortion."

But neither Viki Wilson's story, nor equally tragic ones told by other women, persuaded the members of the U.S. House — including the six men from Oklahoma — who proudly and resoundingly voted a ban on what they pointedly call "partial birth abortions."

The ban forces women into life-threatening situations and the doctors who would perform this and other procedures to face up to two years in prison, monetary fines or both. It's the first time the U.S. House has voted to ban some abortions since *Roe. v. Wade* was decided and the first time ever the government has tried to ban a specific medical procedure.

The procedure at issue is called intact dilation and evacuation (D&E). The phrase "partial birth abortion" is an incendiary invention of abortion opponents that does not appear in medical dictionaries or in textbooks. In the bill, its definition is completely vague — many doctors don't know what the authors are talking about.

As with all late-term abortion, D&E is, indeed, a grisly medical procedure.

"The procedure is done typically," reports the L.A. Times, "only to avert an outcome as gruesome as the operation itself — the death of the woman — or to remove a severely deformed fetus that would not survive after birth."

Proponents of the ban whipped up a hysterical frenzy over the procedure, which involves partial extraction of the fetus into the birth canal and collapsing the skull in order to extract it. But, in fact, all of the options for terminating late-term pregnancies are gruesome. D&E is the safest. In an ugly attack on women, abortion foes circulated bloody photos of the procedure, claiming they were commonly performed.

The truth is, D&E accounts for only about 200 of the 1.5 million abortions performed annually in this country, and the demise of the fetus — a fetus, remember, so severely deformed or ill it will die soon after birth — occurs in the womb.

Opponents of this ban understand exactly what this chilling attack is all about: It is another attempt to paint them as baby-killing monsters and then, ultimately, to ban all abortions. One California congressman gleefully referred to the bill as "the beginning of the end for abortion rights."

What a cruel way to shove a political agenda down our throats. Beyond the scare tactics of morbidly describing this procedure that no one would wish on any one else, where is the popular support for this? A majority of Americans, including Oklahomans, still believe abortion should be legal in cases where the life of the woman is at stake. And most people also believe decisions about abortion ought to be left up to a woman and her doctor, not a woman and her congressional delegation. How hypocritical that the most vehement critics of government intrusion would dare use that same government's authority to supplant the judgment of women and their physicians.

"What is clever about this new visual tack of the anti-abortion leaders," wrote Boston Globe columnist Ellen Goodman, "is that any late-term abortion is gruesome."

"What is malicious about this attack," she wrote, "is that it's aimed at families that wanted babies, at women whose pregnancies went terribly awry."

What is also clear is that if Oklahoma's U.S. senators, Don Nickles, R-Ponca City, and Jim Inhofe, R-Tulsa, vote for this ban, too, they will be signaling greater concern for furthering their own political agenda than in saving the lives of women.

EPILOGUE

Oklahoma's two U.S. senators did vote for the ban, along with a majority of the members of the Senate.

President Bill Clinton vetoed that legislation and a similar bill in 1999. Subsequently, many states, including Oklahoma, passed similar measures banning late-term abortion. But in the summer of 2000, the U.S. Supreme Court found Nebraska's so-called partial-birth abortion law unconstitutional in Stenberg v. Carhart. *Among other things, the Court found that any such measure must include protection for the pregnant woman's health, a provision not included in the Nebraska law. Based on that 5–4 decision, the laws in 29 other states that ban late-term abortions are most likely unconstitutional and unenforceable.*

MAKE ABORTION AVAILABLE
JANUARY 1998

I n 1963 — my junior year in high school and a full decade before *Roe v. Wade* was decided — my mother handed me a newspaper article about a teen-age girl in our home town who died trying to end her unwanted pregnancy by inserting a pair of scissors into her own womb.

"Please, please," my mother said. "Come to me if you're ever in trouble like this. I promise I will help."

How lucky I was to have a mother who, in spite of abortion's illegality, had the courage to talk about it and to let me know she would stand up for me in spite of the taboo surrounding it. But while she was offering invaluable support, she was promising something she probably couldn't have given me then or now, even after 25 years of legal abortion. Today my right to a safe abortion is certainly legal, but it is a right that is almost impossible to exercise.

In the Fifties and Sixties, the number of illegal abortions performed in the United States may have been as high as 1.2 million, including 5,000 deaths annually. Before Roe, untrained or unethical medical workers, friends, husbands and boyfriends of pregnant women or women themselves tried to end their pregnancies using dangerous methods like throwing themselves down stairs, drinking Drano, douching with Lysol or inserting objects into their wombs like an umbrella, plastic tubing, a garden hose or the now infamous coat hanger.

By making abortion legal in Roe, the U.S. Supreme Court did not invent the surgical procedure. But since Roe, while the number of legal abortions has not increased significantly, their safety has. In 1991, there were only 11 known deaths in the entire United States from almost 1.5 million legal abortions.

The U.S. Supreme Court's decision in Roe was arguably the most important day for the health and safety of women in my lifetime. With Roe, women could make the decision to end dangerous or unsupportable pregnancies within the privacy of their own homes, doctor's offices and consciences. And doctors were finally free to perform those procedures safely and legally, without fear of legal reprisal.

So what's the problem? The most conservative Court in 50 years has embraced and reaffirmed Roe; poll after poll shows that a huge majority of Americans want to keep abortion safe and legal; and for eight years, we have had a president, Bill Clinton – the first since Roe was decided – willing to take a strong pro-choice stand.

But make no mistake about it: In the trenches, where it counts, in clinics and doctor's offices, the radical anti-choice right is winning. Abortion may be legal, but can you get one? Not easily. At the crux of the matter is a question asked by writer Jack Hitt.

"Can people be said to possess a right if they're too afraid to exercise it?"

Through intimidation, fear, financial threats, clinic bombings, violence and even murder, anti-choice fanatics have driven away all but a few abortion providers. In two clinics and just a handful of offices in central Oklahoma, there are only a few physicians who will still perform abortions and only 2,000 left in the entire United States.

Today, Planned Parenthood of Central Oklahoma can refer patients to only three reputable physicians in the state for a safe abortion. It is virtually impossible to get a first-trimester abortion in any hospital in the area. And while there may be individual physicians willing to perform procedures on some of their private patients, they won't talk about it.

Of those 2,000 doctors who will perform abortions, nearly 59 percent are 65 or older. For them, abortion is not about politics or morality; it's about safety. They were in medicine before Roe, when young women arrived at hospitals near death from self-induced abortions.

Their initial encounter with abortion was not as a political argument or an agenda item in an HMO liability committee meeting, but as an emergency. These doctors go on providing abortions because they know they are saving lives.

"I respect these people who have picketed outside my office for 25 years," one doctor told The New York Times.

"But I know what would happen if they were successful politically — a lot more tragedy, a lot more deaths. We have saved ... hundreds of thousands of lives."

These courageous practitioners do their work in a kind of "medical shadowland," where doctors wear bullet-proof vests, and security guards patrol their clinics, and sometimes their homes, 24 hours a day.

Today's medical community of frightened physicians, medical school and hospital administrators, mostly unfamiliar with the horrors of illegal or unavailable abortion, is reacting, in part, to the argument that abortion is immoral; they are bowing to financial and political pressure. They don't even teach abortion in medical schools anymore. As one local gynecologist told me, "They're chickens."

It's understandable. If your practice — indeed, your own safety and that of your family, your patients and employees — is at risk, it's understandable that you might be unwilling to perform abortions. Let someone else do it, you say. Let residents get their own training. Let patients go elsewhere. Not in our emergency room. Not in our hospital. It's understandable, but not acceptable.

What are frightened women and girls to do? What if you live in Ardmore, Okla? There are no providers there. Can you afford the time and money to travel here or to Dallas? What if you wait for your Medicaid check and by then, it's your second trimester? You certainly can't afford an abortion now.

I offer a challenge to the medical community. While it may no longer be possible to mandate medical training for abortion, administrators and faculty can make it easier for those who want the training by offering a curriculum that teaches safe abortion as an option and a response to the need for indigent care. It is a legal option for patients and should be one physicians can offer them. I challenge you, too, to use your collective power as physicians before hospital and HMO committees, before anti-choice groups and with law enforcement to provide women a safe, medical option they are entitled to have.

It is daunting, but it is still possible to get an abortion in Oklahoma, and women are not yet taking extreme measures to end their pregnancies. But will they, when they can no longer find a doctor to provide one? Will they when they cannot drive to another state or country? Who will help our daughters and their daughters when this generation of doctors that "still remembers" isn't around, but hasn't been replaced because no one knows how to do their work or has the courage to try?

EPILOGUE

Since this column was published, there has been good news and bad for women who want to choose safe and legal abortion.

In October 2000, the U.S. Food and Drug Administration finally approved the use of RU-486 in the United States, an oral abortifacient (medically induced abortion) already available to women for many years in Europe. Supervised by a physician, the series of three similar medications is given to a pregnant woman at several week intervals prior to seven weeks of pregnancy. It is not inexpensive, so poor women continue to be deprived of this option. But it is safe, private, and now, legal. Doctors who, for whatever reasons, do not perform surgical abortions are increasingly willing to prescribe RU-486.

But accessibility to surgical abortion remains a growing problem, and abortion opponents using violent tactics are largely to blame. In 1999, Dr. Barnett Slepian, a private practitioner in upstate New York and the father of young children, was murdered in his home by anti-

abortion advocates who proudly claimed the action in the name of what they call their holy war. Another serious threat to accessibility to safe and legal abortion are religious-based hospitals who require doctors and medical personnel to pledge not to perform the procedure in their facility.

Roe, itself, has been threatened and could be overturned, as it hangs in the U.S. Supreme Court by a margin of one or two votes on most cases. With the election of George W. Bush as president, and hints by several Court justices of retirement, the right to safe and legal abortion is threatened again. It is an issue the American people consistently believe should be left up to women and their families and an issue the Congress and state legislatures continue to use to stack up political points.

A CITY IMMUNE TO SUFFERING
JANUARY 1995

PROLOGUE

In December 1987, German Swastikas and anti-Jewish epithets were painted on the walls of both Jewish houses of worship in Oklahoma City, Temple B'nai Israel and Emmanuel Synagogue. During the same month, a cross was burned in the front yard of an African-American church. Two young men were arrested for the acts of vandalism. There was a significant cry of outrage in a town largely unaccustomed to seeing that kind of malice directed toward its religious institutions.

Oklahoma City Council Member Mark Schwartz responded to the incidents by proposing a hate crimes ordinance for the city and establishing an accompanying Human Rights Commission. The ordinance outlawed intimidation and harassment; damage, destruction or vandalism of real or personal property and assault and battery because of a person's race, color, religion, creed, ancestry, age, sex, sexual orientation, ethnicity, national origin or disability. Both the ordinance and the establishment of the commission were approved by the Oklahoma City Council in March 1988.

The volunteer Human Rights Commission considered complaints filed by individuals claiming violations of the ordinance primarily in the area of employment harassment or discrimination.

The Commission had no prosecutorial or subpoena power, but served effectively as a mediator in more than 30 cases of employment discrimination, often helping parties resolve their conflicts away from the public eye and away from the legal system. The group referred even more cases that were beyond its reach to the appropriate departments in the state and city, such as the city attorney's office, housing office, police department, state Human Rights Commission, etc.

In 1993, the U.S. Supreme Court found a similar hate crimes ordinance in St. Paul, Minn., unconstitutional, and a revised ordinance was proposed by Commission members to the Oklahoma City Council for its consideration.

Then the trouble started. The Daily Oklahoman — not having paid much attention to the commission's work for six years — suddenly noticed that the ordinance and the commission included the protection of gays and lesbians, among others. The paper editorialized against passage of the ordinance and served as a rallying cry for fundamentalist religious groups who packed City Hall to oppose it.

Some religious organizations in the city, such as First Stone Ministries, whose mission is primarily to teach and preach against the so-called sin of homosexuality and to "convert" homosexuals to heterosexuals, were the most vocal. It was the weight of this faction — both in numbers and volume of antipathy — that, according to Schwartz, "started a firestorm in this city."

I have a good friend who is living with and will soon die from AIDS.

He's too young, too talented, too kind, too much fun and too important to our community to die so soon. He is gay and has spent his entire life trying to understand who he is and then fighting those who hate or fear him because of it. So I hope you will understand that at this point I'm pretty fed up with anti-gay bigotry.

His sister — a religious woman, a wife and the mother of two small girls — told me, "This disease has given us all an immune deficiency syndrome of the heart. We can no longer ignore the suffering of others."

But this week, a majority of the Oklahoma City Council again voted down a human rights ordinance that would protect minorities, including gays and lesbians, from discrimination, leaving me to wonder if many on our council are themselves immune to the suffering of the living.

While they give lots of excuses for not wanting this ordinance, let's be honest here: Most of those voting against the ordinance do not believe gay people are entitled to the same protection from hate, harassment or intimidation as others. Busloads of people showed up at the meeting to say that they, God and Jesus are positive about homosexuals being evil, and they don't plan to waste their time or money worrying about these people's rights or even safety.

Some of their excuses are these: Homosexuality is some kind of lifestyle choice, they are so very sure, and an immoral one at that. They even paraded some "repentant homosexuals" before the council to prove it.

Or they hide behind the excuse that our business community will be hampered by asking employers to be fair in their hiring practices.

Or they say it's unfair to protect homosexuals from harassment over say, heterosexuals. Or this not-so-hidden agenda: Some want to see colleagues on the council — who are their adversaries on other issues anyway — live or die politically defending "those queers." Or in the reverse: They want to use their opposition to including homosexuals in the ordinance as an issue for their own political gain, as in, "Not me, buddy; I'm not for those queers."

Or maybe they really are immune to the pain, fear and anger felt by all minority populations singled out for ridicule or left out of the main.

Maybe Council Member Jack Cornett, and others, have never been called a fag or a kike or a nigger or a redskin by someone nasty and mad enough to do them harm. (Mayor Ron Norick, in support of a proposed separate hate crimes ordinance that would strengthen assault and battery penalties if motivated against someone because of his minority status, did speak eloquently about this.)

Or maybe opponents of a human rights ordinance have never been frightened that three skinheads in a pickup would leap out of the truck and hit them with a club, screaming queer or faggot. Maybe they've never been fired because they were too old or their last name was Gonzalez or they recently moved here from Vietnam but haven't yet become proficient in English. Maybe no one in their family was dragged out of their home and killed because of who they are and what they believe.

These things should never happen to anyone, but they do. All the time, all over the world. And here in Oklahoma City, America, with the notable exception of a few members, the very men and women elected to preside over the rights and responsibilities of every citizen refuse to take a stand against this same kind of bigotry and intolerance.

Maybe they think it isn't necessary. Maybe they will go on thinking of these men and women as gays first and human beings second. There is no law requiring them to call upon their humanity and respond to the injustice done against gay men and women, living or dead. They do not have to treat these people as they would wish to be treated themselves.

In fact, if they don't, they'll probably get more votes.

EPILOGUE

The Oklahoma City Council ultimately voted 6–3 against the revised ordinance. Seeing that the battle had been lost, but wanting to preserve at least some semblance of an anti-discrimination policy for the city, supporters of the ordinance finally agreed to drop gays and lesbians as a protected group. But by this time, pressure from anti-gay groups had worked against certain members, and a majority voted to abolish the Human Rights Commission entirely.

EIGHT

WHAT MATTERS MOST

NO MORE VACATIONS
JANUARY 1996

ome years ago, possibly when then-Attorney General Robert F. Kennedy was conducting an all-out war against organized crime, the federal government began paying key witnesses to spill and split; i.e., to go away. Far, far away, as in, poof. Disappear. Evaporate.

Called the Federal Witness Protection Program, the idea is to protect people who know really bad things about really bad people but are too scared to say so. So in exchange for testifying, the government provides them a new identity, re-locates them and pays them until they find a way to support themselves, legally, one presumes.

I want to join. Now.

Forthwith I will spill, then I want to split, slipping surreptitiously and unceremoniously into another identity, another locale, another career, another life — because I am so fried, so bushed, so plumb tuckered from The Holidays that everyone and everything in my path needs protection. I am a little too close to organizing some crimes of my own.

Whether disguised as Mommie Dearest or spirited away in a plain ol' yellow cab, it doesn't matter. Just get me the hell out of wherever and whoever I am until I can rest up and am no longer a witch to those I love and homicidal to those I don't.

Does anyone else feel this way? Has anyone, like me, come back from a long, lovely holiday more exhausted than before you left? Why, after the Big Holiday Build-up and then the Big Holiday Vacation followed by the Big Holiday Vacation Let Down, do I now need a break from home, hearth, job and all other forms of demanding life? Even though my holiday took me to a heavenly spot where I had great fun, saw wonderful friends, ate delicious meals and had lots of good times with my family, I came home frazzled, finished and otherwise pooped.

So frazzled, in fact, that everyone and everything – from my slimy, dead pansies to my sweet, harmless dog – are really at-risk around me. Except for snapping at everyone, I am unable to do anything except rent mindless movies and fantasize about packing a very small valise, leaving a note on the door – "Gone out for lox and bagels" – and vaporizing.

And I need to get gone quickly, because the breaking point is near. Get me out before we have one more day of below freezing weather; before anyone else in my house gives me a hard time about writing thank-you notes or sleeping 'til 1 p.m.; before there is no more choco-late left to eat because I've eaten the entire international supply for two years. Lemme out! Before I am forced to streak up and down the street to work because none of my clothes fit. Hurry; I'm winding down to a shrieking halt.

The requirements for my new life are simple: No one will know my name or any variation of it – not Pam not Mom not Honey not Associ-ate Editor Fleischaker not Mrs. Fleischaker. I will answer to no one because I will be no one.

I must be located where my phone number and address are unat-tainable because none of the other inhabitants of, oh, say, Beachbliss Bay will have phones or addresses, either. In Beachbliss, appliances won't break, New Year's cards are never sent, and everything fits so you never have to exchange anything.

The temperature will never rise above or reach below 75 degrees; the breezes will be gentle and balmy; appropriate dress is cut-offs, a T-shirt and $1.69 flip-flops. KJ-103 and pro football are banned. Sched-ules and deadlines are unheard of; fat grams must be left at the border; there are no flights in or out, especially on United Airlines. No one can run for office, change parties, call for a congressional investigation or coach a basketball team.

As for those of you who signed up early on to hang with me

through thick, thin and all that, you can come along, if and only if you have no agenda other than a beach chair, a margarita, a trashy novel, mounds of fresh fruit and seafood served by bronzed, blue-eyed beach boys with no brains. You must go along with lots of sleep, athletic activity in the boudoir only and no — under any circumstances — absolutely no vacations.

A PASSOVER PRIMER

*W*e're beginning to get ready for Passover at our house, the Jewish holiday celebrating the ancient Hebrews' freedom from slavery in Egypt.

This is the historical basis for the holiday, but for me, Passover is actually a celebration of the matzo ball, and thank God for that, because what's a holiday without *schmaltz*[1]?

But now you ask: Aren't all holidays filled with plenty of schmaltzy, warm emotion? Yes, *shmendrick*[2], but at Passover, the schmaltz (two tablespoons, melted) is mixed in with six eggs separated, a cup of matzo meal bought, some salt and pepper and after a little of this and a little of that, you have matzo balls.

Schmaltz is a Yiddish[3] word for chicken fat which can't be avoided at Passover, and who wants to anyway. Jews have a tendency to run high cholesterol, which, considering schmaltz, chopped liver, cheese blintzes[4] and *kugel*[5], is easy to figure.

The story of Passover is the story of a great struggle for freedom. For years, the Jews in Egypt had been doing lots of heavy lifting for one of the big Pharaohs who was a miserable excuse for a leader and the first in a long line of tyrants. That was followed, finally, by an exodus and 40 nightmarish years of wandering through the desert with not much more to eat than matzo (unleavened bread), which looks

---

[1] Rendered chicken fat (Grandma says to make it really tasty, render it in a good pot with some onion.)

[2] A dunce; someone for whom no one has any use; a term without gender but rarely applied to a woman

[3] A language derived from a combination of Hebrew and German and my mother-in-law's first language spoken in her home in Enid, Oklahoma.

[4] Russian pancakes stuffed with cheese, fruit or better yet, both

[5] A delicious noodle pudding

like road-kill Wonder Bread left out in the sun to dry and doesn't taste much better than it looks unless you spread lots of butter on it, which brings us back to the cholesterol problem.

There are many important things about Passover, but for me, none so important as food. For each significant event that befell us in The Days of Old, there is a delicious dish to symbolize it, eaten with much explanation and fanfare at Seder, the Passover dinner and service. Besides, what's a celebration without racking up a few more triglycerides? Gluttony is my point.

Jewish tradition actually speaks to gluttony at Passover. Because slouching was prohibited in Egyptian bondage, the Seder is to be enjoyed from a reclining position.

Personally, I interpret this thusly: After four helpings of chopped liver and six leaden matzo balls in chicken soup, reclining is all you can manage. I also recommend wearing a trench coat or tent, so you can fill up without having to loosen your pants or skirt in the middle of the meal, which is endless with lots of praying and arguing *in mitn derinnen*[6].

In fact, I have never attended a Seder when an argument didn't break out over whether Jews in America are too much assimilated, whether Uncle Moishe was really a socialist or just grumpy, whether we should be sending more or less aid to Israel, whether most hotel bathtubs are clean enough for bathing or that age-old debate: Whether the best matzo balls should be light and fluffy or hard enough to lob into enemy territory.

My favorite dish among the traditional ones is *charoses*, a mix of chopped apples and pecans, cinnamon and Passover wine. Yes, from the great vintners Mogen David and Mr. Manischewitz come two of the worst wines ever squeezed out of the *nebuchal*[7] grape, but either is plenty good enough for cooking.

[6] Loosely translated, "in the middle of everything, this too?"

[7] Pathetic. Actually, worse than pathetic.

Charoses is served as a symbol of the mortar and bricks the Jews were forced to make for those *fahrshtunkinah*[8] Pharaohs and their pyramids. The work was hard in those days, but eating charoses with homemade horseradish spread on a piece of matzoh is a *machiah*[9]. If you want to try it, or the almighty matzo ball, call me for the recipes, but don't expect much in the way of exact measurements. As Sara Kasdan wrote in a cooking classic, "If one spoonful is good, so two is better!"

If you only have time for a shortened version of the Passover Seder, my friend told me recently about a prayer that works for all Jewish holidays.

"They tried to kill us. We won. Let's eat."

Whether your choice is matzo balls at Seder or a honey-baked ham for Easter Sunday brunch, I say *L'chaim*[10] to you.

And may you know peace, freedom, a few words of Yiddish and a case of indigestion worth every bite.

[8] Bad, smelly, rotten, rotten, rotten

[9] A true pleasure

[10] To life!

MILLENNIUM MADNESS

JANUARY 2000

or nearly one year, my family planned our millennium celebration. No airplanes, no airports, no dependence on air
traffic controllers. No huge crowds. No risky hub cities. No
computer-run subways or mass transit systems.

No exorbitant hotels or crowded restaurants. No muss, no fuss. Just
a pleasant drive west to our favorite get-away in New Mexico and an
at-home celebration with family and closest friends.

Ah, friends. Ah, family.

You can't live without 'em and you can't kill 'em.

Ultimately, we pulled it off — 14 people and two dogs, huge dogs,
spilling out of one small, rustic mountain house and a borrowed
apartment. Well, eventually two borrowed apartments, having something to do with too much closeness, too little comfort.

And it was monumental; madly and millennially monumental. We
had lots of home cooking, lots of blazing fires, lots of music, games,
hikes, excursions, newcenturyspeak and oldcentury reminiscences.
Martha (Stewart, of course) would have been proud. We used lots of
Her recipes and talked a lot — doesn't everyone in this century? —
about Her new IPO.

Our ages ranged from 7 to 84, with several stops for adolescence,
post-adolescence and menopause in between. But, above all, it was kin
and kissin' kin, and after 10 days I'll put our challenges up against any
Y2K emergency grid center anywhere.

We had two cases of the flu, sequentially, complete with emergency
room visits and meals on wheels; a long, steep driveway made impass-
able by snow, but only one unplanned fire in the kitchen. We lost car
keys, a lot of money to a locksmith, a cart of groceries, a shuttle bus,
cell phones, jackets and an airplane ticket.

Alternately, and in descending numbers of years, we lost our patience with crowdedness, clutter, wet towels on the couch, dogs in sleeping bags, clogged toilets, ski slope lift lines, restaurants slow to handle 10 or more of us at one sitting, rowdy grandchildren, kids on the phone, kids online, kids spread out everywhere.

Early on New Year's Eve, we visited the home of other friends and their family. They had a beautiful cocktail party in a clean house with well-dressed and smiling children. Oh God.

After that failure-by-comparison, we went home, and I lost it over dirty laundry on the dining room table and how long it took to carve the damn roast. My husband grumped over the treasured and long-saved bottles of Lafitte-Rothschild wine now turned to fine French vinegar. Grandpa lost it over rude and disorganized grandchildren; sisters out-bossed each other in the kitchen; friends out-shopped each other. Nobody knew who was going where or in which car or by what time. Tempers flared, teeth gritted.

Y2K bugs? Hell, this crowd's been buggin' each other for years and have passed some of these same bugs along to family and friends all our lives. Some we've worked out, some we haven't. But above all else, we were here, for and with one another, and I wouldn't have been anywhere else.

We tossed crappy Mylar confetti high in the air, popped corks, drank champagne out of even crappier plastic flutes and watched a bunch of joyous revelers in Times Square, all of us squeezed around a borrowed 7-inch television screen. Then half of us went to bed and didn't mind a bit, and the other half did whatever you do after midnight when're so carefree that nothing bugs you.

Our vacation wasn't perfect, but neither are we, my family and my friends.

Happily, most people seemed to have passed the millennium mark much the way we did — with a lot of anticipation and chaos mixed with laughter, muss and fuss, after all. Yes, there was a little grousing and a few snafus, but no bugs so big or momentous as to disrupt the most common, central and cohesive bond in all of our lives, our family and our friends.

Corny it is, but as it turns out, we are one for all, and all for one. And here's to all of us.

UNVEILING THE POSSIBLE
MAY 1991

 few days after my mother died, a wise friend said eventually this would all become part of my history. I could not believe that.

Nearly all day every day for months, I felt that an essential part of me had been torn away, that I was badly broken, not at all whole, and was standing, if at all, on either side of a trembling, quake-like crevice. This feeling was so pervasive, I couldn't imagine it ever giving way to acceptance of her absence and my loss. This is it, I thought. I have lost my mother, my source, my center, myself.

My friend guessed this acceptance would begin to happen around the time of the unveiling of my mother's grave stone, a Jewish ritual held more or less one year after a death. This custom derives pragmatically, as do many things in Judaism, from ancient practices. Jews once buried their dead in open fields, moved on in their nomadic culture, waited a year for the natural process of decomposition, then returned and removed the bones, burying them finally in ossuaries or underground caves.

Throughout those months, the official period of mourning went on, but not until the final burial in the ossuary did the mourning end and the permanent markings were made in stone at the burial site. Today we modify this custom and, after a conventional funeral, wait a year to unveil and erect a gravestone.

For me, the year has been in some ways a gift, in some ways a necessity and in another way, a kind of command. I expected sadness and sorrow, but I also unrealistically expected that I, a modern and in-control-of-my-emotions kind of woman, would grieve and then finish grieving. I did not, and I have not.

I needed the year and will need more. I'm grateful there has been this time of allowed, almost prescribed grieving. My misery has not only been sanctioned, it has been expected.

It is 20th century folly to tell yourself that your mother is gone, but since everyone loses someone they love, you can get over this. The ragged emptiness may give way to a milder, more easily mended pain, but this is not something you get over.

Still, this unveiling is also a command for me to get on with the business of living my life. It is not possible to do that, I think, if you have not had time to feel death.

For the last year, it has been my mother's illness and death that has haunted and surrounded me and almost become my own story.

Now as we lay a stone beside her grave, marking both the spot of her burial and the end of one phase of mourning, I feel I am unveiling, finally, the possibility of making her rich, full life, and not just the pain of her death, part of her story and my history.

WHAT MATTERS MOST

MAY 1999

hroughout the evening of May 3, 1999, when the now-infamous F-5-rated, quarter-mile wide, powerful, deadly tornado struck Oklahoma City, my daughter and I watched television weather reporters very carefully. The precise locations of intersections predicting where the twister was headed next and its exact arrival times at those streets, were flashed on the screen accompanied by the increasingly tense voices of meteorologists. As we began to recognize areas on the maps and names of familiar nearby neighborhoods, the announcer warned all of us in Oklahoma County to seek shelter.

OK, we said, looking at each other with a little fear and a lot of determination. Seek shelter we will.

We live in a close-in downtown neighborhood, built in the twenties, and most of the houses, including our own, have basements. Yes, we were jittery, but I reassured her. After all, that's a parent's job, isn't it? Reassure them even when you haven't a clue if what you're saying is true.

"What matters," I said, "is that we are safe and together."

"And we will be safe in the basement, so let's get going."

Down we went, hauling flashlights and batteries, a few candles and some matches, a couple bottles of water, a portable phone, portable television (more batteries), some blankets and pillows, homework (her priority, not mine, but, hey, I was impressed) and of course, the dog.

After setting up shop, I remembered all my stuff. Like a high-tech scanner, my mind ran a fast inventory over the house — my things, my husband's things, the kids' things. Things everywhere. Years and years worth of things brought back from special travels. Things from birthdays, knick knacks, dresses, baubles and beads.

Should I worry about the computers or cars or VCR or my husband's new stereo? Nope, not now.

Clothes, jewelry or the great shoes I just bought on sale? The hell with them. How about the furniture, rugs, china? Nope. Don't care.

Oh, gosh. Paintings and books and Grandma's keepsakes. Nice, if there were time, but there's not.

I looked around me in the basement, and suddenly none of that mattered much. If all of it were all blown off the face of the earth this very night, would it really matter?

For a lot of people, everything they owned was blown off the face of the earth that night. I hope they survived with the people they cared about, and, sadly, 44 people in our city did not.

Everything that mattered to me was right there with me. Everything else was replaceable. Not easily, not cheaply, not without dislocation and loss. But really, none of it counts. I told myself, I have my family, my trusty dog and my memories ...

"Photos!" I said to my daughter, with a new sense of urgency. "I want the pictures!"

"And my journals," she said to me. Her growing-up life, day by day, since she was a young girl.

So back up we went, dashing frantically through the house, grabbing photo albums, pictures in frames, pictures off walls, diaries, travel journals, baby books — everything that helped us remember how and where we'd lived, how we'd looked and who had been there with us.

No matter how much we shop and spend and collect and stash and store, memory is all we own. And post-50, I've noticed I don't own as much of that as I used to, so photos and chronicles are a must.

As we watched the growing storm, fearful for those to the south and east of us, we were lucky. Piled up together in the basement looking at years of memories — "God, Mom, how could you have worn your hair like that!" and "Yes, you definitely were a goofy looking baby" — we had all we needed.

Dishes break. Furniture wears. Cars rust. Computers become obsolete. Shoes stink. Clothes get too tight. Jewelry fades. Flowers die. Hours fly. Things pass by. They can all be blown away. But love stays.